REASON *to* BELIEVE

Answering the Toughest Questions About God

HR HUNTSMAN

HUNTSMAN PUBLISHING

Reason to Believe

ISBN 978-0-9862273-0-1

Published by:

Huntsman Publishing

Foreword

I have a friend who is a very successful businessman. Emphasis on very. And when he calls me and tells me that he has met a leader and a thinker who is a "Jesus guy" and tells me how this leader has really impressed him, I pay attention. That is what happened to me several years ago, when I first heard about HR Huntsman. He is a community leader and a thoughtful and articulate forerunner of a Jesus movement that is impacting our community, the country, and even the world. I could not be more excited about a pastor and leader than I am about my friend HR. You will feel his personality and intellect as you read these pages. I know you are not able to know him the way I do, but you can learn from his years of studying the Scriptures and helping people really "get it." Enjoy! You are in for a treat! When you pick up this book, you are beginning an adventure. It will stimulate your intellect. It will equip you and make you wise. It will give you confidence in who God is and what he is capable of doing through you. This book will be a blessing to both people who have no faith and to people who have nurtured their faith for many years. In fact, you might want to save yourself a trip to the store and buy a second copy for a friend right now.

—Dean Curry

Acknowledgements

I have so many to thank for helping me bring my first book to reality.

Self-publishing a book is a very expensive endeavor, and I had so many great friends make donations to make sure this project was completed at the highest level of excellence. I am forever in their debt. Special thanks to: Ray & Sandy Fraley, Bill & Lola Thwing, Jerry & Germaine Korum, Dan & Nancy McLaughlin, Gayla Goetze, John & Jody Holmes, Lew & Rose Lewis, Dale & Leslie Peasch, John & Nadine Simmons, Jamie Smith, Rob & Lyn Barrow, Diana Sims, Brad & Sandy Bradbeer, Steve & Joan Wehmhoefer, Britt & Teresa Stockrahm, Rob & Jackie LaPlante, Hugh & Rayna Messer, Joe & Jessica Bard, Nicole Wirth, Graham & Bobbi Northcott, and David & Cynthia Froembling.

Robyn Harai was a tremendous help for my first round of editing, as well as an invaluable advisor to help this publishing newcomer learn how to bring a book to life. I could not have done this without all her help.

The incredible staff and congregation of Real Life Family Center. You are my friends, my family, and my encouragers and your belief in me inspires me. Your constant question, "When are you writing that book?" made sure this project never died. I would never have finished without all of you believing in me.

My wonderful son, Nate, who constantly makes me proud as a father. I would love to have been as solid as you are at the same age. Keep growing, my son.

My daughter Danielle, who also works as my publicist, was an invaluable help in helping me promote and publicize Reason to Believe. You are the best daughter any daddy could hope for.

Finally, my amazing wife, Gwen, who is my biggest fan, greatest supporter, and the light of my life. There are no words to express the depth of my love for you. Your constant question, "Are you writing today?" was a loving challenge to keep this project moving forward. Reason to Believe would not exist without you. I would be far less of a man without you.

Contents

REASON *to* BELIEVE

Answering the Toughest Questions About God

Introduction

"Question what every teacher tells you!" This was the educational advice given to me by my mother. It was repeated on many occasions, often with her traditional vim and vigor thrown in for good measure. My mom was born in 1934, and was a throwback to the stereotypical pioneer woman. She was a mother of nine boys (that alone would force a woman to be tough :) and as hardnosed as they came. She was a straightforward, "in your face," no-nonsense kind of person. She never gave or took excuses. She was an accomplished, wiry six-foot athlete and musician in high school, but had suffered a great amount of personal loss and heartache. By the time I came into the world, this had cemented her attitude and outlook on life. At times, she was brash, opinionated, loud, and harsh. She was a hard worker, a hard drinker, and could be a hard mother. At other times, she was incredibly generous, kind, and gentle. If a person truly needed help, she would give the shirt off her back. If you betrayed that kindness or acted the fool...well, don't say you weren't warned.

Although many other men would later come and go, my dad was the closest to a father figure — and he couldn't even remember my name. The first stroke took his memory when I was a year old. Though we lived in the same house, I didn't know he was my father. I didn't understand why he couldn't remember who I was or where his bedroom was. I had just told him yesterday, "Second door on the left." He taught me how to ride a scooter and swing on a swing, and then his life was cut short. The second stroke took him from me when I was just nine. There were many men, but my mom was the one constant — good and bad. I've had to overcome many of the negatives of my upbringing and tried to embrace much of the positive. One of the many positives that stuck with me is her outlook on education. "Question what every teacher tells you!" She wanted me to push the bounds of knowledge with every teacher I had. "Make them work," she would tell me. It wasn't enough to know the facts of the Boston Tea Party for a test. I was to know *why* the colonists acted in the manner they did. She wanted to make sure I knew how to learn. She didn't just want me simply swallowing any and all information that some teacher gave me, but also to learn how they got to that conclusion and whether it stood the test of further inspection. This attitude of questioning authority was hardly rare at this time. I was born in the mid-sixties. This was a tumultuous time for the United States. We were in the middle of the Vietnam War, the sexual revolution, the civil rights movement, and Watergate was right around the corner. Challenging authorities was the rule of the day.

The Pink Floyd song "Another Brick in the Wall" sums up the mentality of this period.

We don't need no education
We don't need no thought control
No dark sarcasm in the classroom
Teacher leave them kids alone

Hey teacher leave them kids alone
All in all you're just another brick in the wall
All in all you're just another brick in the wall

As for me, I was not brought up to disrespect authority, simply to question it. This was not questioning for questioning's sake, or to play the rebel, but to simply learn how to gather, process, and embrace information—to think.

As I matured, so did my questions. Basic questions about history, math, and grammar grew up into questions about life, our existence, the nature and origin of the universe, and religion. This was beyond the three *R*'s of education (by the way, why does only *one* of the three *R*'s begin with an *R*? Doesn't that signal a deeper problem in our education system?). This was deeper stuff. How did we get here? Heck, how did *anything* get here? Is there purpose, or do we just live and die…like amoeba? Those questions began to gnaw at me and I began to pursue the best answers I could.

That's what this book is about. I've taken those principles my mom tried to instill in me and applied them to life. Whether it was in the high school classroom, in the military community, in college, or on the job, I've continually asked questions. (By the way, the military does not look very kindly on young recruits asking a bunch of "why" questions.) The content of this book is formed around nine basic questions—Tough Questions. These are questions about creation, evolution, religion, morality, consciousness, science, and eternity.

I'm sure you have noticed the subtitle of this book is not "Answering the Toughest Questions," but rather, "Answering the Toughest Questions about *God*." The reason for that is simple—that is the ultimate question. Either there is a Supreme Being, or power of some sort, or there is not. The following nine questions are set in a specific order and are meant to lead the reader down a logical path from creation through life's origins to questions about consciousness, religion, and salvation.

Now, some would say that the answers to these questions are unknowable and asking them can only lead to the endless debate of mere opinion. I disagree. For each of these questions, there is an abundance of logic, evidence, and even common sense based information that can help the critical thinker come to a reasonable conclusion. And while we may not have the "concrete proof" that a scientifically oriented society would prefer the simple fact is that much of what we believe is not based on "concrete" or scientific proof (I will get to specific examples of this in later chapters), often times the best we can do is settle on the answer that has the greatest chance of reasonable certainty.

What qualifies me to write this book? I am not a scientist, nor a theologian, nor a philosopher. I hold no advanced degree in any of the fields related to the questions in this book. I am just a common man…with questions. I have read dozens of books and hundreds of articles in my own search for answers. I'll simply share what I have learned with you and leave the decision about my answers you. I have been told that I have a knack, a gift perhaps, of being able to communicate complex matters in a way that's easy to understand. That's what I hope to do in the next few pages.

I won't even begin to pretend that my questions are uniquely profound or that my answers are my own. I have simply gleaned them from much more powerful thinkers than myself and am trying to pass them on to others in a way that makes sense and connects well.

Now, there will be some who read my answers to these questions and want to charge me with being biased. So, let me address the subject of bias up front. Of course I am biased. Every writer is. The better question is, *why* is an author or speaker or teacher biased? Is it simply out of stubbornness or ignorance, or is it because he's been diligent and open-minded in his search for answers and has come to what he believes are logical conclusions because of that journey? Any person who has wrestled with hard questions, and has come to reasonable conclusions while remaining open to new information, *should* be biased. As the old saying goes, "If you don't stand for something, you will fall for anything." My question is, "Is what I'm standing for at all solid or reasonable?"

Who is this book for? This book is written with two primary audiences in mind.

My main audience is skeptics and seekers. I can very much relate to that inclination, and in some ways I still count myself among that group. I find nothing wrong with healthy doubt and skepticism. Those powerful agents drive my personal quest for answers. If the matter at hand, in this case the existence and nature of God, can't bear the weight of my scrutiny, then it should be jettisoned. If, however, my intellectually honest questions lead me to a greater understanding of life, creation, and purpose, then that skepticism and doubt serves me well. It is far better to be an open-minded skeptic than to never ask the question in the first place.

I also hope that Christ followers will read this book and find a stronger foundation for their faith. The Christian faith is hardly "blind," as some assert. There are numerous solid reasons to embrace it as a worldview, and we will uncover those in this book. A well-informed and educated Christ follower is much better prepared and equipped to help others discover the most powerful message of hope and restoration the world has ever known. The vast majority of Christ followers have not been trained to think critically. This is apparent in our churches. There seems to be a vague notion of faith and belief, and even some agreed-upon belief points, but when questioned with "Why?" the average believer has no answer beyond, "I just believe." In a skeptical and pluralistic society, this answer will no longer suffice. It never should have. There are good, solid reasons for belief in the God of the Bible, and Christ followers owe it to themselves to discover and be able to explain what those are. Please, take the time. Do the hard thinking necessary to educate and train yourself to defend your faith with gentleness and clarity.

I've read dozens of articles and books on the scientific subjects addressed in the following pages. I have done my best to make these concepts as easy to understand as possible. However, it's impossible to avoid them all together and they may be foreign to some readers. Go slowly, read, and reread difficult sections. Look up unfamiliar words and concepts. Learn! You'll be glad you did.

Before we begin, I'd like to say a little about the order of the nine questions. I've put them in what I consider a logical order, from the beginning of the universe to the discussion about Jesus as God. Others might put the questions in order of most asked. In my experience, that would put, "Why is there so much pain?" at the top of the list. Even though the questions are layered in a logical sequence, there is nothing wrong with jumping to any question that you might be more emotionally connected to. If that's the case, I would then advise you to go back and revisit all the arguments that built up to that particular question.

With that being said, I'd like to invite you on a journey of discovery. Using questions as our vehicle, we will explore the outer reaches of the universe and the inner workings of the cell. We will explore the power of reason and logic as well as the credibility of ancient documents and eyewitness testimonies. As we answer those questions, we'll be able to come to solid and reasonable conclusions that will help us form a defensible worldview. Thank you for joining me on this journey. Let's begin.

—HR

Question 1

Why Does This Even Matter?

CHAPTER 1

"Three days later they finally discovered him in the Temple, sitting among the religious teachers, listening to them and asking questions." LUKE 2:46

"If one sets aside popular assumptions and beliefs about what a "god" is or wants and instead starts from a neutral position, then it's not obvious that the existence of some god is necessarily important."

FROM THE ATHEISM.ABOUT.COM WEBSITE

THE JOURNEY BEGINS. WE WILL be looking through telescopes and microscopes. We will be discussing the incredible power of the formation of the universe as well as the mind-boggling complexity of a strand of DNA. Our topics will range from astronomy to biology to philosophy to plain old common sense. You may likely agree with some of what I'm saying, and you may passionately disagree with some of it as well. Following this, we have eight remaining questions that will lead us from the Big Bang to the Empty Tomb, but I must start all the questioning off with, "Why?" Why does this even matter? Why even bring up God? Why discuss, discover, dig, or debate? Why not just forget the whole matter entirely and go about our lives without ever addressing the God question? I submit to you that not only should we not ignore this question, but, in fact, it is the most important question we could ever possibly ask—and attempt to answer.

There are only two possible realities. Either God exists or He doesn't. Either we are the product of His imagination, or He is the product of ours. Each of those possible realities has monumental implications. Let's look at each.

There are only two possible realities. Either God exists or He doesn't. Either we are the product of His imagination, or He is the product of ours.

WITHOUT GOD, LIFE IS ABSURD

"I observed everything going on under the sun, and really, it is all meaningless—like chasing the wind." This was the observation of one of the Bible writers at a time of hopelessness and despair in his life. If there is no God, then his statement is not just the product of depression, it is reality. It is a fact. Think about it for a moment.

Without God, the universe is unexplainable. Without God, there is no cause or intent or explanation for the universe. It just is...and is doomed to death. The universe has a finite life span, and scientists predict that when it runs out of energy (and it must), it will eventually be cold, dead, and lifeless. No stars to emit heat. No galaxies spinning. No planets orbiting. Nothing living. Everything dead.

Without God, life is an accident. You and I, and everything thing that lives, are just an amazing, incredible, biological accident. Chemicals just happened to spill onto one another at the right time, in the right amount, in the right conditions, in an otherwise incredibly hostile environment and somehow, life emerged. Eventually, millions of years and billions of mutations later we have...you. Another cosmic accident.

If there is no God, then death is the end. There is no heaven, no afterlife, no beloved relatives waiting for us "on the other side." There is no other side. This is it. You scrape and claw as many years as you are able to squeak out of this cosmic accident and once your lights go out, well, you are done and another accident is there to take your place. Does that sound bleak? Of course it does, because it is. That's simply the reality of a godless, random, accidental universe. What are the implications of such a reality? There are three significant ones we should look at: Value, Meaning, and Purpose.

Value

I was a juvenile delinquent. In a chaotic home, and without a strong father figure, I was left to my own for much of the time. Greg was my best friend and next door neighbor and had a similar home life. We quickly formed a dynamic duo of elementary age havoc. On a free summer afternoon, we threw rocks through the windows of Buena Vista Middle School. I remember one Sunday morning, we woke up with a particularly devilish scheme and planted nails on the side of the road where we knew the "Joy Bus" would stop and pick up kids to take them to church. Operation "Flat Tire" didn't work. I still don't know why. We thought it was pretty foolproof. At the core of all our mischief was shoplifting. Sporting equipwment, transistor radios, and lots of candy were our favorite targets. Over the years, we honed our craft of thievery. We learned it's pretty easy to stuff your pockets with hard candy, but that approach is tough with a baseball bat. Trust me, I tried. So we put our devious minds to work and came up with a plan—switch the price tags. Back before the days of UPC codes, sticky price tags marked the value of an item. We would simply take the price tag off an inexpensive item and put it on the item we wanted. The only wrinkle in the plan was the checkout person. We always scoped the checkout stands and aimed for the just-out-of-high-school-girl, who probably had no stock in the business and didn't know or care about the item in question. We got bats and mitts and radios for pennies on the dollar. The value of the item became whatever price tag we desired to place on it. Without anyone of authority there to challenge it, the value became whatever we decided. We felt so powerful.

A world without God is also a world without any intrinsic value. The traits we call our "values" are simply manufactured from thin air and have no real basis. Compassion, generosity, heroism, and integrity are nothing more than facades we create and, in reality, have no worth whatsoever. In fact, life itself has absolutely no value. How can it? In a world without God, where everything that lives is an accident, and the universe itself is doomed to die, this value we call "life" is nothing more than a lie we tell ourselves. In a world without God, there is no reason to rush into the burning building to save a trapped child. She will die anyway. There is no reason to protect the innocent from harm or abuse. The abused has no more value or worth than the abuser. In the absurd world without God, we are simply handwriting these falsified price tags and attaching them arbitrarily to anything we please, but ultimately nothing has any real worth at all.

Point to Ponder

If there is no God, then what basis do we have for giving value to people or life itself?

In a world where there is no God, we may not like or agree with the price tags others choose, but we have no basis to insist they change. For the "good" of mankind? There can be no such thing as "good." Everything we call "good" is nothing more than a fake price tag. This is an absurd way to live and, in fact, we cannot live that way. In Tough Question #6, we will explore this further as we ask, "Why Do I Care?"

Meaning

While value has to do with worth, meaning has to do with significance. Since a world without God means life has no real value, then it follows that life would also have no meaning. Just as we must arbitrarily assign value to random traits, we also attempt to assign meaning to our otherwise meaningless lives.

For a seven year stretch, I lived in Eugene, Oregon while I was pursuing my education following my service in the Air Force. I spent a great deal of time on and around the University of Oregon (Go Ducks!). UO students, like those on many major college campuses, are very cause oriented. On any given weekend, you can expect to see picketing or demonstrations or signs promoting one cause or another. While one group is trying to save the old growth forest, another group is raising money for Greenpeace, while yet another is railing against the evils of fur or greenhouse gases or oil spills or... you get the idea. What do all these causes represent? Meaning. These students are simply looking for a way to say, "My life matters. Listen to me. I am significant." Are they?

Point to Ponder

Why do you think that many who don't believe in God still look for a larger cause?

Not if there is no God, they're not. Each of those causes is in vain. Why save the whales, the forest, the fur seal, the ozone, or anything else if it's doomed from the start?

Who is to say that serving the leprous poor in Delhi is a greater use of a life than selling crack to school kids in Harlem? Unless there's some standard of significance by which we can measure a life, then any attempt we make at assigning meaning is futile. To argue for significance and meaning in a universe that has no God is absurd.

Purpose

I love mountains. The smell of ponderosa pine, the sight of a herd of elk, and the incredible view of the Milky Way on a clear night all bring great joy and peace to my soul. I can feel my muscles relax, my mind clear, and a smile cross my face. While I love to spend alone time in the forest as a way to refresh and re-energize, I also love to introduce the beauty of the woods to others. During the summer of 2013, I had the opportunity of taking a small group of hikers around the challenging, but spectacular, Wonderland Trail. The WT is the 94 mile loop that circumnavigates Mount Rainier. Over the past decade, I've enjoyed the great accomplishment of summiting Mount Rainier seven times. In the last three years, I've also had the wonderful challenge of leading groups of twelve to sixteen climbers in summit attempts. Summiting the tallest peak in Washington State, and the most revered alpine summit in the lower forty-eight, is far from easy. Rainier is *tough*! Steep, icy slopes in twenty degree weather in the middle of the night, with the danger of crevasses at every step for twelve straight hours, are not for the faint of heart. Many times during the climb, I've asked myself, "Why am I doing this again?" The answer is simple, "To stand on the top of the State of Washington and help others stand there as well." There is a purpose. So I, and others, put one foot in front of the other despite the cold, the exhaustion, the hunger, and the monotony because there is a greater purpose. You see, the view from the summit is incredible. The feeling of accomplishment is unbelievable. The sunrises are extraordinary. So we push through, or maybe better said, we are pulled along—by a greater purpose.

Purpose is reason lined with hope. It's why we work long hours, endure difficult relationships, or sacrifice for our kids. We feel there is a nobler, grander, greater purpose. But, wait! If there is no God, then there is no reason, no purpose, to pull us along to persevere so we can stand on mountain tops. It's like climbing a mountain with no summit to stand on, no accomplishment to revel in, and no sunrise to witness. You just keep climbing and climbing and climbing...till you die. To argue for purpose, that life has intent and direction, in a universe without God is absurd.

Value has to do with worth, meaning has to do with significance, and purpose has to do with intent or direction. Purpose is the overall grand view, the big picture, and the ultimate reason. Undoubtedly, you've picked up by now that in the absurd world without God, none of these things is possible. Life is ultimately worthless, meaningless, and purposeless.

God Changes Everything

After reading the above, you're thoroughly depressed. If you cling to the notion that there is no God, then you should be. The universe is doomed to death and all life to extinction. There is no real value, meaning, or purpose to anything we do, or the very life we live. We are a cosmic, chemical, and biological accident and nothing more. However, *if* there is a sovereign, uncaused, timeless, personal, good God, then that changes everything.

If there is such a being, then life has value, because now there is an objective value system outside of our own by which we can measure worth. Life has meaning as well. It's not enough for life simply to be valuable; it also needs to have significance. Otherwise, I'm a valuable person, but the legacy I leave may not be. If God is timeless, then maybe the meaning and investment of my life can be important and significant after I'm gone. With God also comes purpose. If God is eternal, then maybe, just maybe, my meaningful and valuable life also has a greater, grander, nobler purpose as well. Can it be that our reason for living goes far beyond the seventy or so years we see lying in front of us? Does purpose laced with hope keep us putting one foot in front of the other as we head toward our own personal summit?

I would suggest that a universe with God in it makes much more sense than the absurdity of life without God.

Nothing is More Important

I am not suggesting that the absurdity of a universe void of God proves that He exists. It doesn't. Maybe life really is that empty of value, meaning, and purpose. What I am suggesting, however, is that we cannot, we must not, avoid the question. We're beginning this journey of discovery with the question, "Does this even matter?" Should you, the reader, spend another moment of your time asking these questions and looking for evidence that helps you decide

Can you think of a more important question than whether God exists or not?

one way or the other? Yes! A thousand times yes. These are the most important questions you can possibly ask.

Questions about the existence and the nature of God are the most important questions one can possibly ask. Either He doesn't exist and life is a valueless, meaningless, purposeless accident, or He does exist and has a grand and noble purpose for your one and only life. All the other pursuits in life pale in comparison to answering, or — at the very least — earnestly attempting to answer this question. You bet this matters! Nothing matters more.

We've settled the question of importance, so let's begin the exciting journey of discovery. If God exists, has He made it possible to discover Him? I look back at history and I'm amazed at the passion for discovery that seems to be hardwired into humanity.

We have sailed seas, crossed continents, climbed mountains, learned about the body, walked on the moon, and examined the ocean floors because of questions. We always seem to be asking, "Why?" or "What's over there?" or "How is that made?" I wonder if that passion for discovery was given to us by our creator so that we could enjoy an exciting adventure that brings us to find Him? All those great adventures and discoveries were launched by questions. Ours will be as well.

We'll begin our question inspired journey by looking through the telescope as we ask, "Why is there something rather than nothing?"

Question 2

Why is There Something Rather Than Nothing?

Chapter 2

"In the beginning, God created the heavens and the Earth." Genesis 1:1

"I believe in God, only I spell it Nature."
Frank Lloyd Wright

It was a huge step for our growing family. I was in the eighth grade and we had just made a major move. My mom, newest step dad, and the four of us boys made the journey from Carrizozo, New Mexico, up the mountains to Ruidoso. My parents had just sold the six gas stations my mom had acquired over the years and purchased a very large new station and mini mart in this quaint tourist town. Ruidoso is a beautiful little village nestled in the southern tip of the Rocky Mountains, and it is known for its skiing and quarter horse racing. I spent most of my early childhood years around gas stations as my mom, a single mother, built up a small empire of stations and mobile homes, from which the operators of these stations could live. These were all full service, and I spent countless hours pumping gas and checking the oil and tire pressure of our customers. I clearly remember having to wash windows while standing on the crate that our milkman brought our milk in. Those days were now gone, and my folks had put all their eggs into the one basket of this large self-service station. "Self service" and mini marts in gas stations were a new cultural trend at this time, and ours was the first of its kind in town.

I remember this particular year not only for the move, but also for my fourteenth birthday gift—a telescope. I had asked for, and received, a 300x power Tasco telescope. I couldn't wait to peer into the deepest recesses of the heavens. I wanted to know what was out there. Could I view powerful black holes, sucking in everything nearby? Or possibly new galaxies being formed? Perhaps supernovas in mid-explosion? Sadly for me, I discovered that a 300x telescope barely gets teenage boys much past the moon.

For the record, no matter how often my wife tries to point it out, I still can't see the "Man in the moon."

Over thirty years later, we're now seeing the images sent back by the Hubble telescope, and many of us gasp in awe and amazement at the beauty, the magnitude, and the scope of our universe. Astronomers have come up with wonderful, but less than creative, names to describe these magnificent discoveries. The spiraling "Cat's Eye" nebula, the elongated "Cigar" galaxy, and my favorite, the towering "Pillars of Creation." As it turns out, there is *so much* out there. But the larger question remains. Exactly where did it come from? It's not enough to simply find it. Don't we need to explain it, or at least try? The mere existence of the universe demands an explanation, or at least an investigation! How did it get here? How did *we* get here? These questions have been asked countless times since...well, probably since we've been able to ask questions. As you can imagine, the answers to these most important of questions vary.

I've discovered that the answers can be put into 3 major categories.

> **The universe is eternal.** It has no beginning and no end. It always has been and will be. It just — is.
>
> **The universe is self-existent.** It is not eternal, but has a beginning and simply sprang from absolute nothingness all by itself.
>
> **The universe was created.** There is an external creative force or mind outside of, and independent, of the universe.

We'll explore each of these views, and then you can decide which is most credible and reasonable.

Explanation 1
The Universe is Eternal

Until just a few decades ago, this was the predominant worldview held by many outside of religious circles. There are some today, like Bertrand Russell, who still hold to this view. "*The universe is just there, and that's all.*" [1]

While certain religious texts, like the Bible, speak of an omnipotent creator, most non-theists believed that the universe was eternal. Throughout the Renaissance age of the fourteenth through the seventeenth centuries, there was a rebirth of intellectual thought. On the heels of the Renaissance dawned the eighteenth century's "Enlightenment Period" and a greater emphasis on philosophy, intellectual and scientific curiosity, and reason. As scientific knowledge increased, a disdain for religious thought also increased. Science gained great prominence and promise within the Western world, and an explosion of discovery and innovation followed over the next two centuries.

Georg Ohm's law of electricity (1827), William Morton's discovery of anesthesia (1846), and Gregor Mendel's laws of inheritance in genetics (1865) each greatly affected our understanding of the world around us. Alessandro Volta would invent the electric battery in 1800, Elias Howe the sewing machine in 1846, and Seth Wheeler brought us toilet paper in 1877. Many new scientific discoveries were responsible for great advances in medicine, technology, and industry. We now had the telegraph, automobiles, and cameras. We had begun to better understand the body, the nature of the cell, and vaccinations.

Really? We had batteries before we had toilet paper?

All of these developments gave Western culture a false sense of security in science's ability to explain many things, including our universe's origins. For centuries, mainstream thinking was that the earth was the center of the universe and the universe itself was eternal. And why wouldn't they believe that? There was no evidence to say otherwise. We were told we no longer needed to believe in a omnipotent creator, since we now had such informed insights. We were told we no longer needed the myths of religion. If we couldn't explain something, it was only a matter of time until science could figure it out.

Omnipotent comes from two words.
Omni, meaning "all," and potent, meaning "powerful."

Please don't misunderstand and assume I'm one of those religious wackos who believes that science is evil and opposed to theistic be lief. Hardly! I absolutely admire science and the tremendous benefits it has brought us. I grew up in an irreligious home that prized learning. Many of my Christmas and birthday gifts were science oriented. I spent countless childhood hours with chemistry sets, mixing chemicals and creating putty or spewing volcanoes or, better yet, something that exploded. Later into my junior high years, my interest moved toward erector sets and building miniaturized machines and motors. In my high school years, electronic sets became my fascination. Now I was creating shortwave radios, light activated alarms, and many other projects with my Radio Shack 500 and 1 electronic kit. It was this love of electronics that propelled me into my electronics career in the Air Force. I was a computer programmer and an electronics technician for the B-52 Electronic Warfare Systems. While working toward a degree in electronics engineering, my very favorite class was biology. I was then, and still am now, fascinated by the amazing structure and systems of life. Please hear me clearly when I say that I love science. However, as I've grown, I have also come to realize that science does not have all the answers to many of our most important questions. Actually, science is quite unqualified to address many facets of life.

Many of the things formerly believed by the intellectuals of their time as "fact," such as the world being flat and the earth as the center of the universe, are now known to be false. The eternal nature of the universe is one of those formerly held beliefs that, in the last century, has been shown to be incorrect. In a fascinating twist, it is now science that is proving that the theistic view of the universe is far more probable—the universe had a beginning. The popular name for this beginning of the universe is the "Big Bang." This term was coined by Fred Hoyle in a 1949 radio broadcast to describe the universe's explosive beginning from a single point, which scientists have since labeled the "singularity." At this point, a finite universe exploded into existence, and both space and time came into being out of absolutely nothing. Let's take a look at the streams of discovery that prove, beyond a reasonable doubt, that the universe is finite and had a beginning.

For my own memory, I created and use the acronym **B.E.G.I.N.** to help me remember these five streams of discovery. Let's look at each of them.

B – Background Radiation

(From the initial Big Bang Explosion)

In the early 1900's, as the idea of the "Big Bang" was beginning to catch on in the scientific community, researchers began to postulate and theorize cosmic side effects. This is another example of how good science works. If theory *A* is true, then we can expect certain effects or evidences. This is the Law of Causality at work, and all of science is built on causes. One of the evidences of this violent beginning that scientists began to look for was left over radiation from the initial explosion. *If* the Big Bang was an accurate model, then certainly researchers could find the radiation signatures. And they did.

The *B* in my B.E.G.I.N. acronym points toward the radiation, technically called the Cosmic Microwave Background Radiation (CMBR), left over in the universe from that initial mind-boggling first event. The cosmic microwave background was predicted in 1948 by George Gamow, Ralph Alpher, and Robert Herman and it was finally discovered almost two decades later.

In 1964, researchers Arno Penzias and Robert Wilson noticed a constant pattern of background "noise" they kept picking up on their instruments. They first thought it was interference from bird droppings, but they later discovered one of the most important finds in cosmology. Everywhere they pointed their very sensitive and highly tuned antennas, they picked up these microwave length patterns. They finally realized they were exactly the length one would expect from the background radiation of the Big Bang explosion.

The Law of Causality is the link between effects and their causes. True science continually looks for observable and repeatable causes and effects that reveal scientific laws. More on this to come.

Cosmic background radiation is most easily explained as radiation left over from an early stage in the development of the universe, and its discovery is considered a landmark test of the Big Bang model of the universe.

When the universe was young, before the formation of stars and planets, it was smaller, much hotter, and filled with a uniform glow from its white-hot fog of hydrogen plasma. As the universe expanded, both the plasma and the radiation filling it grew cooler. When the universe cooled enough, stable atoms could form. These atoms could no longer absorb the thermal radiation, and the universe became transparent instead of being an opaque fog. The photons that existed at that time have been propagating ever since, though growing fainter and less energetic, since exactly the same number of photons fill a larger and larger universe.

Precise measurements of cosmic background radiation are critical to cosmology, since any proposed model of the universe must explain this radiation. After many, many verifications, it has become one of the most celebrated finds of all time and adds tremendous credibility to the Big Bang model of the universe's beginning. Penzias and Wilson won a Nobel Prize in Physics for this incredibly important discovery.

Not only does this discovery continue to support the theory of the universe's beginning, but each of the streams of discovery we will examine supports the Bible's description of the universe beginning from nothing. Again, we see world famous scientists noticing this as well.

Robert Wilson, co-discoverer of this radiation afterglow, observed, "Certainly there was something that set it off. Certainly, if you're religious, I can't think of a better theory of the origin of the universe *to match with Genesis.*" [2]

Let's move on to the E in my B.E.G.I.N. acronym

E – Einstein's Math

i.e. The Theory of General Relativity

In 1917, Albert Einstein applied his newly discovered gravitational theory, the theory of general relativity (GR), to the cosmos. When he did so, he found something that he would later call "irritating." (I will address his "irritating" comment in a moment.) His computations predicted that the universe was not static, but in fact must have had an origin. His mathematical predictions in GR told him that all of time, matter, and space had a beginning in the finite past. This theory flew in the face of the commonly held belief that the universe was eternally in a static state. Prior to the 1920's, the idea of a finite and expanding universe was beyond comprehension. Throughout most of human history, the universe was thought to be fixed and immutable, and the idea that it might actually be changing was almost inconceivable.

When asked to summarize the general theory of relativity in one sentence, Einstein replied, *"Time and space and gravitation have no separate existence from matter."* [3] Einstein's mathematical predictions, and the later scientific observations that would prove them to be accurate, rocked the scientific world. These findings go far beyond the scientific community, however. They force the thinking person to ask once again, "Why is there something rather than nothing?" If all of this hasn't existed eternally, but came into existence....how? The answer to that question, and those of the other eight we will ask, are too important to simply shrug our shoulders toward and simply go about our business.

My favorite picture of Albert Einstein is the one where he is sticking his tongue out at the camera. Not at all how I picture a genius scientist.

Let's get back to Einstein's "irritating" comment about his theory. Why would a find, or a discovery, be "irritating" to such an esteemed scientist and mathematician, one of the most brilliant minds in history? Because it violated preconceived values and beliefs. Scientists often try to pass themselves off as completely objective researchers who will only follow the evidence where it leads. But scientists are very human and come to their fields with world views, prejudices, and biases about the nature of things. Einstein later confirmed his theory when he physically observed the universe expanding, as his theory predicted. This discovery, which we will explore in the *I* of B.E.G.I.N., rocked Einstein's beliefs and solidified the fact that the universe is not finite, static, and eternal.

The G in the B.E.G.I.N. acronym has to do with how the galaxies in our universe were formed.

G – Galaxy "Seeds"

My entire family and I enjoy watching good mystery shows and movies. We particularly enjoy American shows, like Criminal Minds and NCIS, as well as the BBC version of Sherlock. We all try to stay a step ahead of the plot and figure out what happened as the fictional detectives methodically pore over a crime scene piece by piece, looking for clues. Some clues are incidental and help build the criminal's profile, while others, like fingerprints and DNA, are far more powerful and can help build a strong case very quickly. Like these detectives, we've been building a very strong case against the idea that the universe is eternal. The discovery of Cosmic Background Radiation and Einstein's mathematical model are very good starts to building a solid case for a temporal and finite universe. There are three more solid clues that will seal this case and bring us conclusive evidence, beyond a reasonable doubt, that the universe had a beginning and is *not* eternal.

After Penzias and Wilson discovered the background radiation we just discussed, scientists reasoned that those ripples in the cooling of the expanding universe would have been instrumental in the formation of galaxies. Gravity would form the cooling matter into galaxy clusters. The search was on.

In 1989, NASA launched the $200 million COBE satellite. COBE stands for Cosmic Background Explorer. With extremely sensitive instruments on board, COBE went looking to see if these ripples existed in the background radiation. In three short years, what they found was truly remarkable. Not only did they find the ripples they were looking for, they discovered that these ripples were incredibly precise, as though they were honed on a razor's edge—down to one part in one hundred thousand. These ripples appear to be precisely calibrated. They are strong enough to allow galaxies to form, but not too strong, which would cause the universe to collapse back on itself. This was judged by Cambridge astronomer Stephen Hawking to be "*...the most important discovery of the century, if not of all time.*"[4]

George Smoot, the project leader, announced COBE's findings in 1992 and could hardly have been more enthusiastic. He gushed, "If you are religious, it's like looking at God," and what they found are "*Machine marks from the creation of the universe,*" and even stronger yet, "*The fingerprints of the maker.*"[5] These galaxy "seeds" are not mathematical or astronomical hypotheses—you can *see* them. The COBE satellite took infrared pictures of these ripples and you can find them at COBE's website: http://lambda.gsfc.nasa.gov/product/cobe.

Our fourth piece of strong evidence for the beginning of the universe has to do with its noticeable expansion.

I – Inflating Universe

When I teach classes on this subject, I give all the participants a white balloon and have them draw stars and galaxies on their deflated balloons. I then have them blow the balloons up to demonstrate the Big Bang model. From a beginning singularity, the universe exploded and, like the balloon, every part is moving away from every other part due to the energy infused into the system. If you were on the surface of the balloon in one of the drawn galaxies, you would see every other star and galaxy moving away from you.

This is exactly what Edwin Hubble (for whom the Hubble space telescope is named) saw when he looked into his telescope back in the 1920's. Hubble came to the Mount Wilson Observatory in California in 1919 and began using the largest telescope on Earth at the time. The 100-inch Hooker Telescope helped him see beyond our Milky Way galaxy, which was considered the entire universe at the time. His discoveries radically changed the way we see our universe. Not only did Hubble discover new galaxies, but in 1929 he also discovered what is now called the Red Shift, or Doppler shift, of light. Everywhere he looked in the universe, he saw a red light phase shift.

This light shift proved that every point in the universe was moving away from every other point. The universe was expanding in every direction and away from a point of origin. This was a stunning discovery and was the first observational support for the expansion theory, which had been proposed by Georges Lemaître in 1927. This discovery rocked the scientific world and presents another serious challenge to atheists and agnostics concerning an eternal universe. It was this very telescope that Albert Einstein looked through to confirm his "irritating" General Relativity theory, which we discussed a few pages ago.

If the universe is expanding from a point of "explosion," then it certainly hasn't been expanding infinitely and can actually be traced back to its origin. Logic dictates that if it had a beginning, then it can't be eternal.

Physicists Tipler and Barrow summarize the Big Bang expansion by saying, *"At this singularity, space and time came into existence; literally nothing existed before the singularity, so if the universe originated at such a singularity, we would truly have a creation ex nihilo."* [6]

Ex nihilo is Latin for "from nothing," and has been used by theologians for centuries to describe the Genesis creation event. It is very interesting to see science find strong evidence that this "from nothing" beginning is exactly how the universe came to be.

The expanding universe is further proof that it isn't eternal, since it is obvious that the expanding universe can be retraced to a specific moment where that first explosion took place. That moment is what astronomers call "The First Event," since both time and space were created in that first explosion of heat and light. Without any evidence associated with the earliest instant of the expansion, the Big Bang theory cannot, and does not, provide any explanation for the initial condition of the universe, nor any prior conditions (remember, there were *no* prior conditions because there was *nothing*); rather, it

Absolutely Nothing

I can't begin to wrap my head around the concept of "absolutely nothing." But it's harder for me to wrap my head around everything coming from nothing by itself.

describes and explains the general history of the universe since that instant.

So far, we have four very solid evidence streams that give us strong proof that the universe had a beginning and is not eternal. There is one more piece of evidence and it is the "smoking gun" of the Big Bang proofs.

N – eNergy Depletion

(Yes, I know I cheated on using the N here :)

A story from my daughter's sixteenth birthday party illustrates this very basic reality that we see and experience every day. Our family gathered to celebrate Danielle's sweet sixteen. She invited a large group of friends out to our home. In addition to volleyball, horseshoes, and a barbecue, she wanted a large bonfire to light up the night. As the resident pyromaniac, this task was left to me, and I joyfully accepted the challenge. I spent all day gathering a large amount of wood from our property and stacking it in a perfect teepee shape, just like I learned as a Boy Scout. By the time I was done, I had a wood pile approximately fifteen feet high and six feet in diameter. To ensure that we would have a memorable experience I then doused the entire stack with two gallons of gasoline. We were ready for our own fireworks —Huntsman style.

At the proper time, I stepped up and threw a lighted match onto my creation and we experienced a BIG BANG of our own. The many eyewitnesses later exclaimed that the fireball soared forty feet in the air. I really didn't get a good look at the explosion because the fireball also engulfed *me,* singeing my eyebrows and arm hair and giving me second degree burns on my lower right leg. Whether I should be trusted to ignite bonfire ceremonies is still up for debate. For now, let's get back to what we will learn is the second law of thermodynamics. Since no more wood or gasoline were added to the fire (my wife forbade me), over the course of the evening, what started with a huge fireball began to lose energy and burn down. Eventually, it became a nice bed of coals, and then finally grew cold.

The same principle is true with our universe and is one of the five streams of proof that the universe is not eternal. Our universe cannot go on forever and has not gone on forever. If the universe were infinitely old, it would have "burned up" all its energy an infinite time ago and would have grown cold. Since the universe has *not* grown cold and the energy is *not* all used up, it's very easy to deduce that the universe is *not* eternal.

I've gone on to light many more bonfires, but I now use an extended fuse — a piece of string soaked in gasoline.

Picture again the blown up white balloon that represents the universe that each of my class participants is holding. Not only does this balloon represent the *I* of an inflating universe, but it also helps me explain the *N* of energy depletion and the second law of thermodynamics. The balloon was inflated due to outside energy (the participant's breath). The balloon is a closed system and the pressure (stored energy) on the latex walls wants to match the pressure in the room. In other words, the air wants to get out, and it eventually will. It may take hours or days, but eventually, the balloon will deflate and the pressure inside the deflated balloon will once again be equal to the room. This is the law of entropy. Just like the Huntsman bonfire, just like the blown up balloon, the universe is running out of energy.

> *"The law that entropy always increases holds, I think, the supreme position among the laws of Nature. ...if your theory is found to be against the second law of thermodynamics I can give you no hope; there is nothing for it but to collapse in deepest humiliation."* [7]
>
> —Sir Arthur Stanley Eddington, The Nature of the Physical World (1927)

The second law of thermodynamics in this context applies to the energy in the universe. The universe is a closed system, and there is no energy coming into the system from outside. To be clear, there *is* no outside. The universe exists as an isolated system within absolute nothingness. The second law of thermodynamics, also called the law of entropy, states that the finite amount of energy in the universe is being used up to power the universe. This makes a great deal of sense, since we see isolated systems all the time that run out of power. Alkaline batteries, your car, and even my own body can be used to illustrate this depletion. I can put a fresh set of batteries in my flashlight and begin working in the dark, but over time, the batteries will run out of juice and my flashlight will eventually go dark. I can put gas in my tank, but it will eventually run out of both fuel and spark. Unless I reintroduce energy from a pump, my car is nothing more than a hunk of junk. The same is true with your body. Without fuel (food), your body becomes an isolated system. It will use up its stored energy (some of us have more than others) and then...die. This is the

> *Entropy: A process of degradation or running down or a trend to disorder.*
> Merriam-Webster

law of entropy at work. Eventually, just like my bonfire and your flashlight, the universe will run out of power and go dark.

The second law of thermodynamics, along with the law of causality (which we described earlier), are the most trusted and respected laws in all of science. Russian thermodynamicist Ivan Bazarov gives his view on the power of the second law.

The second law of thermodynamics is, without a doubt, one of the most perfect laws in physics. Any reproducible violation of it, however small, would bring the discoverer great riches as well as a trip to Stockholm. The world's energy problems would be solved at one stroke. It is not possible to find any other law for which a proposed violation would bring more skepticism than this one. The law has caught the attention of poets and philosophers and has been called the greatest scientific achievement of the nineteenth century. [8]

The strength of the second law of thermodynamics alone gives plenty of solid evidence as to the universe's finite nature, but the four other finds which we previously discussed make the finite nature of the universe a fact beyond reasonable debate.

Before we move on, let's go back to my daughter Danielle's sixteenth birthday party for a moment. It can provide a good, albeit imperfect, model for the five evidences of the Big Bang we just looked at.

Imagine for a moment that the beginning of our bonfire was more than a fireball—that it actually blew the wood and debris outward in a violent explosion. The initial blast and radiation left behind by the explosion would have left heat signatures that sensitive equipment could pick up. That is the **Background Radiation** that started our B.E.G.I.N acrostic. Now imagine someone was at the party and caught this Huntsman "big bang" on video. We could play back the big event later and watch as the fireball exploded skyward and burning chunks of wood flew from the fire pit in every direction. Now imagine we rewind the video in slow motion. We could actually retrace the path of all the bonfire shrapnel to its origination point. This is both the *E* and the *I* of our acronym. **Einstein** mathematically predicted there must have been a starting point to the expansion, and then Hubble witnessed the **Inflation** with his own eyes. All you have to do is logically "rewind" the universe, and you can see it also must have had a beginning. Throw in the **N** and you realize the **eNergy** from the fireball will eventually run out. This is the law of entropy, giving further proof that the Huntsman bonfire wasn't eternal, and neither is our universe.

While the second law certainly does not "prove" the existence of the God of the Bible, it does present serious problems to the belief that the universe is eternal. An infinitely old universe simply cannot be powered by a finite amount of power. The Universe has not existed eternally. Period.

The B.E.G.I.N. evidence in summary:

> **B** – Penzias and Wilson looked for and found the Cosmic **B**ackground Radiation one would expect from such an explosion
>
> **E** - **E**instein mathematically predicted that the universe must have a singular origination point. This was later physically confirmed when he personally looked through Hubble's telescope.
>
> **G** – The COBE satellite under George Smoot's leadership found the earliest beginnings of

Galaxies or "seeds" that they expected to find if the ripples from the above radiation were accurate.

I – Hubble discovered that the universe is **I**nflating away from a point of explosion in the finite past. The red phase shift of light shows that everything in the universe is moving away from everything else.

N – Second Law of Thermodynamics…e**N**ergy in a closed system will deplete over time and can't last forever. If the universe was eternal, all of the energy would've been used up an infinite time ago.

The overwhelming evidence about the beginning of the universe led astronomer Dr. Robert Jastrow—who, until his recent death, was the director of the Mount Wilson observatory, once led by Edwin Hubble—to author a book called "*God and the Astronomers.*" Despite revealing in the first line of chapter 1 that he was personally agnostic about "religious matters," he made this comment about the bias of scientists:

An agnostic is one who is uncertain about the existence of God.

"Theologians generally are delighted with the proof that the Universe had a beginning, but astronomers are curiously upset. Their reactions provide an interesting

> *demonstration of the response of the scientific mind – supposedly a very objective mind – when evidence uncovered by science itself leads to a conflict with the articles of faith in our profession. It turns out that the scientist behaves the way the rest of us do when our beliefs are in conflict with the evidence. We become irritated, we pretend the conflict does not exist, or we paper it over with meaningless phrases."* [9]

I personally am very impressed by Jastrow's openness and honesty regarding the scientist's "faith." He states what I've often found to be true when discussing this evidence with atheists. They have an impressive amount of faith.

These biases and worldviews very often color or skew their research, or they simply fail to see what is so obvious to many. I personally have had many debates with "scientific minded" atheists or agnostics who become extremely heated and agitated over my point of view. When I point out an obvious emotional attachment to a viewpoint that has no scientific evidence behind it, I am often met with great agitation and even anger. I, personally, am looking for the answers that make the most sense given the evidence we have. With that in mind, let's continue.

Jastrow reviewed some of the B.E.G.I.N. evidence and concluded, *"Now we see how the astronomical evidence leads to a biblical view of the origin of the world. The details differ, but the essential elements in the astronomical and biblical accounts of Genesis are the same: the chain of events leading to man commenced suddenly and sharply at a definite moment in time, in a flash of light and energy."* [10]

In an interview, Jastrow went even further, admitting that, *"Astronomers now find they have painted themselves into a corner because they have proven, by their own methods, that the world began abruptly in an act of creation to which you can trace the seeds of every star, every planet, every living thing in this cosmos and on the earth. And they have found that all this happened as a product of forces they cannot hope to discover. . . That there are what I, or anyone, would call supernatural forces at work is now, I think, a scientifically proven fact."* [11]

The tide of scientific and mathematic evidence has turned powerfully against the thought that the universe is eternal in nature. We have looked at the B.E.G.I.N. evidence: five solid streams of scientific evidence that point us back to a clearly defined beginning.

The law of causality proves the universe had a beginning. The law of entropy proves it will have an end. These scientific laws prove the universe was created.

Many, like myself, then state that this massive amount of scientific evidence, while not proving God's existence, most certainly makes a supernatural creator a very reasonable cause. I think Jastrow is right; the scientific and mathematic description of the beginning of the universe sounds a lot like the Biblical account.

Others say, "Not so fast." Ok, so the universe is not eternal, but that does not then presume a creator. Isn't it possible that the universe just created itself? With that in mind, let's turn our attention to the second of the three most popular worldviews regarding the universe's origin—the universe is self-existent.

QUESTION **2** *(continued)*

Why is There Something Rather Than Nothing?

Chapter 3

Explanation 2
The Universe is Self-Existent

As wave after wave of scientific and mathematical evidence turns against the age-old view that the universe is eternal, you'd think that many atheists and agnostics would turn and embrace the theist's point of view that the universe was created. Instead, many choose to believe that the universe sprang into existence, unaided by a creator. In other words, it is self-existent. There was absolutely nothing, and then in a flash of unbelievable power and light—poof! A universe was there. Please let that worldview sink in for just a moment. From *absolutely nothing,* and the next thing you know—*everything that there is* springs into existence — by itself. Astronomer Quentin Smith comments, "*The most reasonable belief is that we came from nothing, by nothing and for nothing.*" [1]

Really? How is *that* the most reasonable? When have you or I ever experienced or witnessed something just appearing out of nothing? Ever?

Now, I freely admit that no one can prove that this did not happen. As we have noted above, this is outside the realm of true science. It is neither observable nor reproducible. However, we don't need science to tell us this viewpoint is weak. All we need is logic and reason— oh, and some common sense coupled with experience. For that appeal to reason and logic, let's examine the age-old Kalam Cosmological argument.

The Kalam Cosmological Argument

The Kalam (pronounced kuh - luhm) argument was named for the Kalam tradition of Islamic discourse. The term "cosmological" comes from two Greek words. "Cosmos," meaning "universe," and "logos" meaning "study of." The Kalam argument, which can be traced to Aristotle, was refined by Al-Ghazali, who influenced the Christian thinker Thomas Aquinas. For over a thousand years, this simple argument has been used to counter the claim that the universe is self-existent. Until Einstein's projections and the subsequent findings that prove the universe had a beginning, atheists could take refuge in the "knowledge" that the universe was eternal. Now that the universe's beginning is a scientific fact, we must look to explain the cause. *Every* event must have a cause. As we noted before, this is the Law of Causality and is the backbone of all science.

We are going to refer to this strong, long-standing deductive argument to explain how the universe can't be self-existent. Before we do, let's review what a deductive argument is.

All deductive arguments have a premise, an observation, and a conclusion.

> **PREMISE** — Everything hangs on the premise being correct. If the premise is faulty, then the conclusion will be faulty.
>
> **OBSERVATION** — The observation needs to be accurate for it to support the premise.
>
> **CONCLUSION** — The conclusion has to neatly and logically connect the premise and the observation.

There are several ways a deductive argument can go awry and lead to a false conclusion. For example:

> **PREMISE** – I like the color black.
> **OBSERVATION** – Crows are black.
> **CONCLUSION** – Therefore, I like crows.

Here the premise and observation don't necessarily support the conclusion. I merely stated that I like the color black, but that does not lead to the fact that I'm fond of everything that is black in color. The premise and conclusion are unconnected and the leap to the conclusion is too large.

Another weak argument:

> **Premise** — All cheerleaders eat ice cream.
> **Observation** — Julie is a cheerleader.
> **Conclusion** — Julie eats ice cream.

The premise here is most certainly false. I don't need to interview every cheerleader on the planet to know I would find at least one that doesn't eat ice cream. I'm quite sure there are lactose intolerant cheerleaders. If the premise is faulty, then the argument is weak.

With that in mind, let's take a brief look at the ***Kalam Cosmological Argument*** and each of those components a little more carefully to make sure it's a sound argument.

> **Premise** — Everything that has a beginning must have a cause.
> **Observation** — The Universe had a beginning.
> **Conclusion** — The Universe must have a cause.

Premise — Everything that has a beginning must have a cause.

This is an airtight premise that has never been be violated. Once again we revisit the law of causality. This is one of the most respected laws in all of science. The terms "causal" and "causality" come from the root word "cause." As in, reading too many scientific articles on physics *causes* me to have a headache. Or, there is a *causal* relationship between how many chocolate chip cookies I eat and how much my weight goes up. It is simply the law of cause and effect. All of science is based on the law of causality. Causes and their subsequent effects are the very foundation of science. The realm of true science is limited to those things which are *Observable* and *Reproducible*. This is the scientific method many of us were taught as early as junior high.

From the Oxford dictionary: "*The scientific method is: a method of procedure that has characterized natural science since the 17th century, consisting in systematic observation, measurement, and experiment, and the formulation, testing, and modification of hypotheses.*"[2]

Francis Bacon, the father of modern science, stated, "*It is rightly laid down that true knowledge is knowledge by causes.*"[3]

The key ideas here are observation and reproduction and those are both based on *cause*. To suggest an effect — the universe springing into existence — without any cause is completely outside the bounds of science and is nothing more than baseless conjecture or, worse, magic.

In a personal letter to John Stewart, then the professor of natural history at Edinburgh, even the great skeptic David Hume wrote, "*I never asserted so absurd a proposition as that something could arise without a cause.*"[4]

Magic shows notwithstanding, no one reading this has ever witnessed something coming from nothing. There is simply no such thing as an uncaused beginning.

Point to Ponder

What would you think of someone who claimed to witness objects appear out of thin air?

We don't drive down the street worrying that a tree will suddenly appear in our path. We don't go to bed at night afraid that we will awake to a giraffe springing to existence in our bedroom. It simply has never happened because it violates the laws of nature. If something began at a point in time, we know beyond all reasonable doubt there was a cause behind it. The premise is solid.

Before I continue with the observation, let me make some comments about electrons in quantum vacuums. While this subject is outside the bounds of this book, it needs to be briefly mentioned here. There are recent observations that some electrons in quantum vacuums appear to spring into existence from out of "nowhere" and then disappear again just as quickly. This "Heisenberg Uncertainty" about these electrons and their origin has led some to believe this is a death knell to the Kalam argument. It most certainly is not. Anti-theists contend that since electrons can spring into existence from nothing in a quantum vacuum, then it's possible that the entire universe sprang into being from a vacuum as well. While I'm not a quantum physicist, I don't need to be one to know that this does *not* violate the Kalam premise.

First, these quantum vacuums have energy all around them. Energy is not nothing; it is something.

Secondly, these quantum vacuums do not exist in nothingness; they are surrounded by a lot of something—namely, a universe. I've had this debate with several people who use this scientific "find" to try to undermine the Kalam argument, and thus the need for a cause for the universe. They argued passionately that these vacuums were surrounded by nothing. Somehow, I could not get them to understand that they are not surrounded by nothing, but exist within a universe. This is radically different from absolutely nothing.

All of science is based on the study of causes and effects. To suggest an uncaused effect is not scientific at all — it's magic.

This is like a person watching a magician pull a rabbit from a hat while denying the existence of the magician and the hat!

Quantum fluctuations do not violate the Kalam principle. It stands solid. With that in mind, we can move on to the observation.

Observation – The Universe had a beginning

We have already seen this observation to be true in the section above. The evidence from our acronym B.E.G.I.N. is overwhelming. While it's true that no one actually witnessed the universe begin, the streams of scientific discovery, mathematical projection, and pure logic demonstrate beyond all reasonable doubt that the universe is finite and had a defined beginning at some point in the distant past. The observation is accurate.

Conclusion – The Universe must have a cause

The premise and observation smoothly and clearly support the conclusion. There is no over-reaching here. Since the universe began to exist in the finite past, there must be a causal force behind it. Though we can't see or explain that force, the simple facts behind the origin of the universe prove beyond a reasonable doubt that there must be one.

Let me close this section by giving a hypothetical example from real life.

Every day, Johnny's dad packs little Johnny's backpack and sends him off to class in the third grade. He makes sure his books are there, homework done, and lovingly packs him a lunch with his favorite treats. One day, little Johnny comes home with a bright orange six-inch rubber ball stuffed in his backpack. As Dad unpacks his son's backpack, he is curious where the ball came from. Johnny replies, "It just showed up, Dad." Well Dad, being a reasonable guy, knows full well it did not "just show up." He continues to question his son as to the ball's origin and explores the likely possibilities.

"Did a friend give it to you?" he asks. "No, Dad it just showed up," Johnny replies.

Dad presses, "Did you take it from the playground?"

Again, "No Dad, it just showed up."

Now Dad realizes that Johnny may not know how the ball got there. Maybe a friend is playing a joke on him or someone stuffed it in the wrong backpack by accident. There are many possible explanations of how the ball got in the pack, but there is one thing Johnny's dad knows, and that is that the ball did not "just show up there." He knows full well that the ball was created in some factory somewhere (probably Taiwan) and somebody stuffed that ball in his son's backpack. Johnny's dad doesn't have to know the identity or character traits of the person who put the ball in his son's backpack to know that *someone, somewhere* put it there.

What's true of six-inch orange balls is also true of universes. The size and scope are different, but the principle is the same. It's astonishing to me that what atheists and skeptics would never believe about orange balls in their child's backpack they readily swallow about their universe. The truth is clear. Our universe did not "just show up." It had an origin and a powerful cause behind it. Let's examine that more fully in our third and final possible explanation for the existence of the universe.

QUESTION 2 *(continued)*

Why is there something rather than nothing?

Chapter 4

Explanation 3
The universe is created

When Einstein made his 1929 pilgrimage to Mount Wilson to look through Hubble's telescope for himself, what he saw was irrefutable. The *observational* evidence showed that the universe was indeed expanding, as his theory on General Relativity had predicted. With his "irritating" belief that the universe was static completely crushed by the weight of the evidence against it, Einstein could no longer support his wish for an eternal universe. He subsequently described the cosmological constant as "the greatest blunder of my life." Einstein said that he wanted "to know how God created the world. I am not interested in this or that phenomenon, in the spectrum of this or that element. I want to know His thought, the rest are details."[1]

Science, math, and reason reveal to us that our universe is not eternal, but in fact it had a beginning. Solid logic, in the form of the law of causality and the Kalam argument, shows us that the universe could not have created itself or simply leapt into existence on its own from pure nothingness. That view violates all reason and our own experiences. That leaves us with one reasonable viewpoint: the universe was created. This worldview is hardly a leap of blind faith, but actually the most reasonable of conclusions. We did not get to this conclusion by examining religious documents, but by examining scientific evidence and using solid philosophical arguments. It just makes sense: that which is caused has a causal agent behind it.

***Contingent** things are things which had a beginning. Logic and science dictate they had a cause. A cause is **necessary** for everything that had a beginning. Therefore, God is a necessary being for the contingent universe.*

The legendary astronomer and mathematician Sir Isaac Newton states what is beginning to appear far more obvious.

> *"Though these bodies may, indeed, persevere in their orbits by the mere laws of gravity, yet they could by no means have at first derived the regular positions of the orbits themselves from those laws. This most beautiful system of the sun, planets, and comets, could only proceed from the council and dominion of an intelligent and powerful being."* [2]

The first tough question we are attempting to answer is: "***Why is there something rather than nothing?***" The only reasonable answer is that there is a creator who caused that it be so. Now someone may leap in here and say, "Not so fast. Didn't you just prove that everything must have a cause? If so, where is the cause for this creator?" I have been asked this question many times by those who feel they have found a loophole in the Kalam argument. They simply are not paying attention. The argument is not "Everything must have a cause," it is "Everything that has a *beginning* must have a cause." Our personal experience limits us to things that have beginnings; we are surrounded by them. We can understand them and explain them. The universe is one of those things. While we may not fully understand its origin or makeup (like Johnny's dad and the nature of the orange ball), we can easily understand the principle.

The law of causality applies only to contingent things and not to necessary beings. A contingent thing is something that had to have a cause for it to exist. The universe is a contingent thing. Because it had a beginning, it must have a cause. A creator is a necessary being. A creator is necessary for the universe to exist.

The supernatural cause of the universe, or creator, is outside of our experience and far more difficult to grasp. The reason we look for natural explanations, even when they are very unreasonable, is because that is what we are familiar and comfortable with.

The idea of a super-powerful, eternal, self-existent, uncaused, timeless creator is challenging, even frightening, to many. It is much easier to put our heads in the sand and ignore the evidence and believe that the universe just is—we are alone and answer to no one. The implications of a supernatural creator can be overwhelming, and

POINT TO PONDER

Why can some embrace the idea of an eternal, uncaused universe but not accept an eternal, uncaused deity?

so the evidence of cause and creation is ignored. I fully understand this reflex, but it doesn't change the evidence at all. By the way, I find it a bit humorous that many are ready to embrace a super huge, eternal, self-existent universe but ridicule those who believe in a supernatural creator with similar traits.

It really boils down to this: is it more reasonable to believe that the universe created itself or that it was created by a supernatural force? It's not at all difficult to extrapolate from our experience that it was created.

Nalin Chandra Wickramasinghe, former atheist Buddhist, is a Sri Lankan-born British mathematician, astronomer, and astrobiologist. He is currently Professor and Director of the Buckingham Centre for Astrobiology at the University of Buckingham. He admits what many scientists are being forced by the evidence to consider:

> *"It is quite a shock. From my earliest training as a scientist I was very strongly brainwashed to believe that science cannot be consistent with any kind of deliberate creation. That notion has had to be very painfully shed. I am quite uncomfortable in the situation, the state of mind I now find myself in. But there is no logical way out of it."* [3]

Science, math, and pure deductive logic can lead us to only one reasonable conclusion: there is a supernatural cause behind all we see. What can we deduce or infer about this creator from what we've learned so far?

The Creator is...

Powerful — this is obvious from the size and scope of the universe — which came from nothing.

Spaceless — because it created space, the supernatural cause must exist outside of space.

Timeless — because it created time, the supernatural cause must exist outside of time.

Independent of creation — this is based on logic and reason. The creator cannot be part of creation that came from nothing. The creator must be outside of and independent of that creation.

Personal—to change a state of absolute nothingness into something requires volition, and volition is a choice. Choices are made by intelligent beings, not by random forces.

The evidence reveals a supernatural creator that is powerful, spaceless, timeless, independent of creation, and personal. This also happens to describe the God of the Bible, which is why I believe in the God of the Bible.

I will conclude this chapter with another classic quote from the agnostic astronomer Robert Jastrow, "*For the scientist who has lived by his faith in the power of reason, the story ends like a bad dream. He has scaled the mountains of ignorance; he is about to conquer the highest peak; as he pulls himself over the final rock, he is greeted by a band of theologians who have been sitting there for centuries."* [4]

This is just the second question and we have already found good, solid evidence for believing in the God of the Bible. We have seven more questions to ask and seven more answers that will reveal this creator even more clearly. With that basic groundwork laid, we can go on to the second question, "Why is there order rather than chaos?"

SECTION SUMMARY

1. There are three basic arguments for the existence of our universe. It's eternal. It's self-existent. It's created.

2. Several streams of scientific and mathematical discovery, the **B.E.G.I.N** evidence, have proven the universe is not eternal, but in fact finite.

3. The Kalam Cosmological Argument is an airtight deductive argument that proves the universe could not have created itself. It demands a cause. The universe is a contingent thing relying on a necessary being to bring it into existence.

4. That the universe is created is the most reasonable explanation for the question, "Why is there something rather than nothing?"

5. The nature of the universe gives us some beginning clues to the nature of this creator. Namely, the creator is: powerful, timeless, independent of creation, and volitional.

Question 3

Why is there Order and not Chaos?

Chapter 5

Evidences of Design

"The heavens declare the glory of God; the skies his marvelous craftsmanship." Psalm 19:1

"The universe is unlikely. Very unlikely. Deeply, shockingly unlikely"
Discover Magazine, November 2000

I couldn't get away from the odor; it hit me like a stiff left jab the minute I entered. It was pungent and thick and seemed to be a mixture of rotten eggs and butane. Though it was almost thirty years ago, I can still picture the room clearly. We entered from an outside covered walkway. The room opened up to the right and approximately twenty workstations filled it. Each workstation had a sink, beakers, pipettes, and a gas outlet to which we would later connect our Bunsen burners. Up near the front of the room, on the left, was the "Chemical Closet." A locked room filled with all the wondrous compounds we would later get to play with…um, I mean learn the unique properties of. This was Mr. Ramsey's domain—junior chemistry class. Mr. Ramsey was a math teacher doubling as a chemistry teacher for a year. He was about as excited for chemistry as most of the students in the class. I, however, was thrilled to put this giant chemistry set to work.

Mr. Ramsey sat at the front of the room and we took our places at stations, clustering with friends. I shared a station with Chris Wynn and Mike Douglas, both of whom were football teammates. Behind Mr. Ramsey was the big green "blackboard," and above that hung the reason for this brief trip down Chemistry 101...the famous Periodic Chart of the Elements. The Periodic Chart displays every element in the known universe, along with its important identifying numbers. The atomic weight, atomic number, and atomic mass are all listed, along with its chemical symbol. The chart lets you know, at a glance, the number of electrons in the outer ring of that element, which then told you what family or class of chemical one was dealing with and how it might react with others.

Periodic Chart of the Elements

1 H																		2 He
3 Li	4 Be													5 B	6 C	7 N	8 O	9 F	10 Ne
11 Na	12 Mg													13 Al	14 Si	15 P	16 S	17 Cl	18 Ar
19 K	20 Ca		21 Sc	22 Ti	23 V	24 Cr	25 Mn	26 Fe	27 Co	28 Ni	29 Cu	30 Zn	31 Ga	32 Ge	33 As	34 Se	35 Br	36 Kr
37 Rb	38 Sr		39 Y	40 Zr	41 Nb	42 Mo	43 Tc	44 Ru	45 Rh	46 Pd	47 Ag	48 Cd	49 In	50 Sn	51 Sb	52 Te	53 I	54 Xe
55 Cs	56 Ba	57-70 *	71 Lu	72 Hf	73 Ta	74 W	75 Re	76 Os	77 Ir	78 Pt	79 Au	80 Hg	81 Tl	82 Pb	83 Bi	84 Po	85 At	86 Rn
87 Fr	88 Ra	89-102 **	103 Lr	104 Rf	105 Db	106 Sg	107 Bh	108 Hs	109 Mt	110 Uun	111 Uuu	112 Uub		114 Uuq				

*Lanthanide series	57 La	58 Ce	59 Pr	60 Nd	61 Pm	62 Sm	63 Eu	64 Gd	65 Tb	66 Dy	67 Ho	68 Er	69 Tm	70 Yb
**Actinide series	89 Ac	90 Th	91 Pa	92 U	93 Np	94 Pu	95 Am	96 Cm	97 Bk	98 Cf	99 Es	100 Fm	101 Md	102 No

Many of you are probably cringing at the thought of the periodic chart. Being forced to memorize the particular numbers and regurgitate them for a test is among the least favorite high school memories for many. Some of them are pretty obvious:

O is for Oxygen, H is for Hydrogen, and C is for Carbon. Some are a bit more challenging: Fe (Ferrum) is Iron, K (Kalium) is Potassium, and Au (Aurum) is Gold.

The periodic chart fascinated me. The amazing and very obvious organization of the elements and how they worked together was the first graphic that really got me thinking about the nature of the universe I lived in. What I could not escape was the order of it all. How all the elements were lined up and placed into groups was remarkable. A skeptic might want to leap in here and shout, "Those groupings and alignments were made by scientists." Certainly the chart itself was, of course, formed by scientists, but they were simply producing a visual aid that reflected how all the elements of the universe actually looked and worked together.

In classic James Bond fashion, the first name of the evil villain in "Goldfinger" is Auric.

I later learned these elements could be put together in predictable patterns to create new compounds. Like tiny little puzzle pieces, they seemed to "fit" together. It all seemed so structured and well thought out, like a microscopic erector set. I was told that the amazing arrangement of the chemicals was all just a wonderful accident. I was told the same thing about DNA in biology class (more about that in the next chapter), but I began to have my doubts. It seemed so well designed.

What began as a teenager's curiosity grew into adult certainty. Some thirty years later, I am more convinced than ever of the design of the universe. That appearance of design goes far beyond the periodic chart I encountered in Mr. Ramsey's chemistry class and extends to even the farthest reaches of our universe.

In the first chapter, we asked the question, ***"Why is There Something Rather Than Nothing?"*** and explored the cosmological argument for the existence of a creator. The cosmological argument simply states that the existence of a caused, finite universe demands an uncaused, infinite creator. But the universe isn't just a big blob sitting in the middle of infinite nothingness. It is more like a finely tuned machine with order and systems and functions. It is this observation of the fine-tuning of the universe that has brought us to our second question, ***"Why is There Order and Not Chaos?"***

When I use the term "Fine-Tuning," I'm referring to the over one hundred laws and forces that enable the universe to produce life on planet Earth. The term "Fine-Tuning" itself is a neutral one and on its own does not imply design. There is virtually a consensus among scientists that the universe itself is remarkably tuned and balanced to an almost impossibly small window of precision in order to produce the life we see. The question is not *if* the universe is finely tuned, but rather, *how* did it get that way?

In order for life to occur, there are dozens and dozens of very complex systems that have to "fit" just so. We'll talk about a few of those in a bit. Before we get into the discussion of design, I'd like you to go hiking with me.

I am an avid backpacker and outdoorsman. I spend a lot of time here in the Pacific Northwest, hiking and climbing around Mt Rainier. In July of 2014, I completed my biggest outdoor adventure to date. I solo hiked 550 miles of the Pacific Crest Trail, beginning at the Canadian border and finishing up in central Oregon. My love for the outdoors began early in my childhood, in the deserts and mountains of New Mexico. I spent my elementary years in the high desert around Alamogordo. My dog,

Scamp, and I would head off into the desert to find riches and adventure. Rattlesnakes, horned toads, scorpions, arrowheads, and unique rocks were among many of the treasures my faithful dog and I discovered. Later, we moved up to the mountains around Ruidoso. There, my backpacking career began in eighth grade, when I joined the Boy Scouts. My best friend, Wade, and I spent countless hours backpacking in the Capitan and southern Rocky mountains. Southern New Mexico is sparsely populated and it was quite easy for two teenage boys to find themselves in the "middle of nowhere," imagining ourselves to be the first explorers in this part of the "wilderness." Twice on backpacking trips in the middle of nowhere we came upon old homesteads. I'd like to invite you to join me on one of those outings.

After thirty days and 550 miles, the bed and food at Timberline Lodge in Oregon was one of the best experiences of my life.

Please imagine that you and I are together in a forest setting. We've been hiking for hours among the ponderosa and white pine. We come upon a clearing and see a large pile of rocks in the form of what looks like a house. Even though it's in decay (see the law of entropy from chapter one), we can easily identify what appears to be the walls, a doorway, two windows, and the chimney stack. You and I are ecstatic to come upon such a find out here in the wilderness and we begin to ponder its origin. There are two possibilities I'd like you to consider. Either the structure, which looks like the remnants of an old rock house, came about by *chance* or it came about by *design*. Which, do you think, is more likely?

Let's look at the chance hypothesis. Is it possible that there was an earthquake some time ago that hurled these rocks onto one another in such a way as to form a structure that appears to be a house? Or, more likely in the New Mexico setting, a rockslide was triggered by gravity or a flash flood and the rocks tumbled down the mountainside and, by freak chance, ended up stacked upon one another in such a way as to form such a structure. Would you really believe that explanation? If I stood there with you, looking at that structure in the wilderness, and tried to convince you that chance and accident were responsible for such a stacking of rocks, how would you respond? You might be tempted to shake some sense into me. You might wonder what you are doing hiking in the wilderness with a person who believes in such fairy tales as house-building-rock-slides. Then you would probably suggest we should be wondering *who,* and not *what,* built that house.

Now let's take a look at the design hypothesis. I think it seems *far* more reasonable that some earlier settlers or homesteaders tried to make a go of it in the difficult New Mexican wilderness. They came upon this clearing, just as you and I did, and decided it was a good place to build a home. They had two building options and chose stone over wood. So these builders began to gather rock from the surrounding terrain and stacked them to create a livable structure. Many years later, due to wind, rain, and snow, the once fully formed house was reduced to walls and chimney. Doesn't this seem like a much more reasonable hypothesis?

Designed things require a designer. I don't need to see the house being built and I don't need to talk to the descendants of the settlers to come to my conclusion. I don't even have to know how to build a rock structure to conclude that it's far more likely that this rock pile that looks a lot like a house *is* a house. It almost certainly was built by a designer and not by a freak rock avalanche, earthquake, or some other mechanism of chance.

What is true of rock structures in the New Mexican wilderness is true of everything, including universes.

> **Premise** — If something appears to have an intelligent design and structure, then it is more reasonable that it has a designer than it happened by chance.

If we can agree on this premise, then the next thing we need to do is see if the universe looks designed or not.

In section one, we looked at the Cosmological Argument as one of the evidences for the existence of God. Basically, this argument says there is a universe and it had a beginning. Since we are quite sure that things can't create themselves, it must have had a supernatural cause.

In this chapter, we'll explore the *Teleological* Argument as the second evidence for the existence of God. Teleological, like Cosmological, gets its meaning from two Greek words: "teleos,"

Cosmological Argument

Everything that begins to exist must have a cause.

The universe began to exist.

The universe must have a cause.

meaning "order," and "logos," meaning study of. Using the teleological argument, we will answer our second question, *"Why is there order and not chaos?"*

In looking at the design, or order, of the universe we must first ask, "What constitutes design?" I propose a simple working definition: "That which reveals intelligence of structure or purpose of composition and would be highly improbable and unreasonable to be explained by chance or accident."

Let's go back to our New Mexico homestead. Only an unreasonable person would try to argue for rockslides or earthquakes as the explanation for the stone home. The broken down cabin is very simple and crude. Still, we know it was designed. The Universe is exponentially more complex, ordered, and precise than that primitive rock home. In the following section, we will look at just five of the roughly 122 precisely ordered forces that have to be in working order for life to be produced on Earth.

Design Evidence 1
Gravity

Several years ago, on a family vacation in Victoria, British Columbia, I found myself on a bridge standing 140 feet over the Nanaimo River. My wife and son waited on the bank below while my daughter stood behind me on the bridge, cheering encouragements. I looked below at the crystal clear water, then I looked to my right at a young man, who smiled and said, "Go." At that command, I jumped! Simulating a perfect swan dive, a huge smile covered my face as I fell freely through the warm summer air. After a fifty foot free-fall the bungee cord began to tighten around my ankles. I continued my descent and then was gently plunged up to my waist into the river. The bungee recoiled, and on my upward arc I shouted with joy. After a few bounces, I was lowered into a raft, unhooked from the bungee, and taken to the bank where my family was waiting. My wife smiled and shook her head. She knows her husband is an adrenaline junkie.

What would cause an otherwise sane forty-year old to plummet 140 feet off a bridge into the river, other than the crazy desire for a rush? Technically speaking – gravity. I merely started the process, and gravity finished the job.

Gravity keeps us stuck to Earth so we don't drift out into space. Most people are probably aware of the legend of Sir Isaac Newton sitting under the apple tree, being hit in the head by an apple, and "discovering" the law of gravity. Gravity doesn't simply pull apples out of trees or forty year olds into rivers or keep us safely stuck to the ground. It's better than that. It keeps everything stuck together. Without gravity, or, with a weaker gravity, our bodies would fly apart, planets could not exist, and solar systems could not have formed. On the other hand, if gravity were any stronger, that would change the rate of the universe's expansion, our sun could not exist, and life could not have formed on our planet. Gravity affects everything: the formation of galaxies, the orbits of planets, the ability of a planet to sustain an ecosystem, and much more. All of these determine whether or not life can exist. The window of opportunity that gravity provides for life is incredibly small. If gravity were altered one way or another, stronger or weaker, by just 0.000000000000000000000 00000000000000001%, then life on Earth would be wiped out.

A slightly lesser gravity is what enables the astronauts on the moon to jump around like NBA athletes.

Is gravity's incredible precision the result of chance or design? If chance, then it's a remarkably accurate stroke of luck for us. The precision of gravity's strength alone is a compelling case for the design argument, but there are several more we will discuss.

Design Evidence 2
The Cosmological Constant

As we learned in Chapter Two, the universe is expanding due to the force of the Big Bang. What is shocking to astronomers is that the universe's expansion speed is increasing the more it expands. The force that causes this is often referred to as "dark energy" or, more commonly in scientific circles, the "Cosmological Constant." The Cosmological Constant is the energy density of empty space. This cosmological constant was included in Einstein's equation for General Relativity and was first assumed to be quite large. It turns out to be much smaller and much more precise than once thought. Robin Collins remarks on this finding. He says, "The unexpected, counterintuitive, and stunningly precise setting of the cosmological constant is widely regarded as the single greatest problem facing physics and cosmology today." [1]

How precise is the cosmological constant? Conservative estimates have it at one part in 10^{53} while others have it at 10^{120}. That is a ten with fifty-three to 120 zeroes behind it. Enormous numbers that represent enormous odds of success. You and I don't have to be mathematicians or physicists to recognize that numbers so big represent either a ridiculously large stroke of luck or intelligent design. The consensus is clear; the cosmological constant is inconceivably precise.

Steven Weinberg, an avowed atheist and Nobel award winning physicist, has commented that the cosmological constant is "remarkably well adjusted in our favor." [2]

My question is, who "adjusted" it? Weinberg goes on to comment on this fine-tuning:

> *"If large and positive, the cosmological constant would act as a repulsive force that increases with distance, a force that would prevent matter from clumping together in the early universe, the process that was the first step in forming galaxies and stars and planets and people. If large and negative, the cosmological constant would act as an attractive force increasing with distance, a force that would almost immediately reverse the expansion of the universe and cause it to re-collapse."* [3]

In either case, if the Cosmological Constant is moved in either direction, there is no universe as we know it and certainly no life on Earth.

Considering just these first two forces, Gravity and the Cosmological Constant, there is a very strong case against chance and a very strong case for design. In fact, astronomer Robin Collins has estimated that just these two forces coming together so precisely, by chance alone, to create life is the equivalent of one atom in the entire known universe. That's quite a long shot!

Design Evidence 3
Carbon Production in the Stars

Stars have long fascinated us. We wish upon them. Sing about them. Make out under them. Ancient sailors and desert travelers were guided by them. For centuries our eyes have been drawn heavenward. Until recently, we had no idea how amazing these twinkling little night-lights were. Stars do more than guide travelers and inspire lovers; they make life possible.

All of life is made possible by the production of, among other elements, Carbon and Oxygen. These two elements are necessary for life to occur. Both of these elements are created in a very precise manufacturing sequence inside stars. Carbon is the foundational element of life, and without it being manufactured in just the right amount, and at just the right speed, life on Earth is not possible. These two chemicals, Carbon and Oxygen, combine to form CO_2 — Carbon Dioxide. Carbon Dioxide, in just the right amount, is essential for life. Carbon Dioxide helps provide the "greenhouse" effect for life. If the CO_2 level were higher, basically a thicker blanket on the planet, there would be a runaway escalation of temperatures and we'd all eventually burn up. If the level were lower, then plants would not be able to maintain photosynthesis and produce the amount of oxygen we need. Without this precise fine-tuning of the manufacturing of Carbon, we are done for. Actually, we never even get started. Have you ever witnessed a well-ordered manufacturing process that didn't have an intelligent mind behind it?

Stars aren't there just to wish upon. They make life possible. Our star, the sun, just happens to be uniquely positioned for life on our planet. Let's look at our amazing sun next.

Design Evidence 4
Our Amazing Sun

The sun is clearly responsible for the possibility of life on Earth. Its light and warmth provide the life sustaining conditions needed on Earth from 93 million miles away. In spite of this, I clearly remember being taught in science class that our sun is relatively ordinary when compared to other stars. Because of its "ordinary" nature, it was thought there must be many more life-giving stars in many more

> *The next time you look up at the sun, think of it as an incredibly well-placed, well-ordered, well-run, carbon production plant.*

galaxies in our universe. Since those days, much more has been learned about the nature of stars and our sun. Technically, the sun is a G2 yellow dwarf, which makes it pretty rare already. Our sun is far more stable than most stars, both in its heat output and its orbit in the galaxy. This keeps our planet in a very safe zone for producing life. As Lee Strobel discovered in his book, *Case for a Creator*:

> *It would take a star with the highly unusual properties of our sun — the right mass, the right light, the right composition, the right distance, the right orbit, the right galaxy, the right location – to nurture living organisms on a circling planet. This makes our sun, and our planet, rare indeed.* [4]

DESIGN EVIDENCE 5
The Incredible Earth

"Who are we? We find that we live on an insignificant planet of a humdrum star lost in a galaxy tucked away in some forgotten corner of a universe in which there are far more galaxies than people." [5]

This very famous quote from the late astronomer and atheist Carl Sagan expresses what many believe to be true. Our galaxy is just one among hundreds of millions. Our solar system is simply a minor one on one of the arms of the Milky Way. Our sun is ordinary at best and our planet…well, just a speck of dust when looking at the universe as a whole. Certainly, as many atheists believe, this must prove that we are not at the center of some grand designer's idea.

When you look at the vastness of the universe and then look at our planet, we do indeed look like a "mote of dust, suspended in a sunbeam" as Sagan also once said. But when we take another look at our planet, a closer look, we discover it's far more special than we thought.

The design evidences of just the earth alone could easily fill an entire book. The earth, and its atmosphere, are a very complex biosphere that functions with great precision in order to produce and sustain life. It was once thought that the universe must have hundreds of thousands — maybe even millions — of advanced civilizations just like ours that have evolved on life-sustaining planets just like ours. Modern science, new discoveries, and fresh thinking are debunking that thinking. As it turns out, Earth is far from ordinary. "Rather than being one planet among billions, Earth now appears to be the uncommon Earth" [6] write Davis and Poe in *Designer Universe*. They go on to say, "The data implies that Earth may be the only planet in the right place at the right time." [7]

Let's look at the remarkable convergence of conditions that create such a "right place" and "right time."

- **Right Place** — The right distance from the right-sized star to receive the right amount of heat and light. Not only are we in the right place in our solar system, but our solar system is in the right place in our galaxy — a "safe zone" in one of the outer arms. Not only are we in the right place in our solar system, which is in the right place in our galaxy, but our galaxy just "happens" to be the right type of galaxy to produce the type of life we see on Earth — a spiral galaxy.

- **Right Size** — A life sustaining planet must be large enough to have the gravity to keep an atmosphere, but not too large for its gravity to pull everything smooth. A smooth planet is a dead planet. We need terrain and mountains or we would be a water world.

- **Right Amount of Water** — Water is needed, but too much water and life stops being generated. The proper interchange of water and land is necessary for life to occur. Our planet just happens to have the right ratios to produce abundant life.

- **Right Atmosphere** — The earth's atmosphere not only protects life from cosmic radiation, but has just the right amount of oxygen, twenty-one percent, to support large brained and muscular life forms. With much more, oxygen fires would constantly erupt and destroy all the vegetation. With much less, oxygen life would suffocate.

- **Right Crust** — We are beginning to learn how crucial plate tectonics are to life on Earth. Ward and Brownlee, in their book *Rare Earth,* state, "It may be that plate tectonics is the central requirement for life on a planet." Plate tectonics not only drive the creation of mountains and continents, which are required to prevent a water world, but they also drive our carbon dioxide cycle, which regulates our greenhouse effect, which is crucial to life. If the earth's crust were thicker, too much oxygen would reach the surface. If it were thinner, there would be too much plate and volcanic activity for life to exist.

- **Right Core** — Plate tectonics are driven by the earth's liquid iron core, which also generates Earth's magnetic field. This magnetic field acts as a protective shield from harmful radiation.

- **Right Moon** — For centuries, people thought there was life on the moon. We now know that the moon itself can't support life. But the moon is key to supporting life on Earth. It's just-right size and just-right distance from Earth keeps our tilt at 23.5°. This stable tilt gives us very mild seasonal weather changes. Without the moon, our tilt would vary wildly, causing our surface temperature to also vary wildly, destroying the possibility for most life forms.

- **Right Rotation** — Much longer rotation and the temperature differences between night and day would be too great. Much shorter and atmospheric winds would be too great.

A graduate from Harvard and the University of Chicago, John O'Keefe, has been awarded numerous honors and is credited with many discoveries in his research while at NASA. In the book *God and the Astronomers,* O'Keefe talks about how astronomy strengthened his faith. He writes the following conclusion:

> *We are, by astronomical standards, a pampered, cosseted, cherished group of creatures; our Darwinian claim to have done it all ourselves is as ridiculous as a baby's brave efforts to stand on its own feet and refuse his mother's hand. If the universe had not been made with the most exacting precision, we could never have come into existence. It is my view that these circumstances indicate the universe was created for man to live in.* [8]

These "Design Evidences" are just a handful of the roughly 122 identified laws and forces that have to be in precise order for Earth to produce life. If just one of them were altered by almost any degree, life on Earth would be impossible. The odds that all these forces came together so precisely by chance is beyond mathematically improbable; it is considered mathematically *impossible*. And yet, here we are. Is it by chance and the freakiest of all possible outcomes, or does this incredibly finely tuned machine called the Universe happen to produce life by intelligent design?

Astrophysicist Hugh Ross calculated the odds that these 122 constants needed for life to exist *anywhere* in the universe by chance is one chance in 10^{138}. [9] That is one chance in 1 with 138 zeroes behind it. This is an enormous number, especially considering two facts: The total number of planets in the universe is estimated at 1×10^{22}. Even more startling is that the total number of atoms in the universe is estimated to be 1×10^{70}. To be blunt, there is *zero* chance that *any* planet in the universe would have the life supporting conditions we have by mere chance. To put these enormous numbers in terms we can better grasp, think of it this way. The odds that Earth produces life by chance are roughly the same odds as standing on one edge of the known universe, firing a bullet, and hitting a target one inch in diameter on the other side.

As theoretical physicist and former skeptic, Paul Davies writes, "If nature is so "clever" as to exploit mechanisms that amaze us with their ingenuity, is that not persuasive evidence for the existence of intelligent design behind the universe? If the world's finest minds can unravel only with difficulty the deeper workings of nature, how could it be supposed that those workings are merely a mindless accident, a product of blind chance?"[10]

Let's go back to our house analogy for a moment. The stone structure you and I stumbled upon had only two building components. The bulk of the house itself was made of rock, with some wood used for the door and window frames. Now let's build a house with five components that represent the five forces we discussed above. Each of these five components is precisely designed and they have to come together in a precise manner and sequence for our house to be built. First, we have a concrete slab. Secondly, log walls are built. Next, cedar shingles are added for the roof. A single, simple metal door gives entry and two windows provide light. There are our five components: Concrete, pine logs, cedar shingles, metal door, and glass windows. I certainly realize that each of those components is made of many elements, but I submit this hypothetical situation for illustration purposes. While this house is far more complex than the stone structure we happened upon in the forest, it's far less complex than our universe, and so it still provides a good analogy.

Teleological Argument

Designed things have a designer.

The universe is very well designed.

The universe must have a designer.

The person who embraces the chance hypothesis of the universe has to believe something like the following for our wilderness cabin. Over billions of years of time, cement came together in powdered form and then, after a freak rainstorm or flash-flood, formed the concrete foundation. Then another few billion years passed as dying pine tree after dying pine tree fell on that square slab and formed ninety degree angles to create the walls. As nearby cedar trees began to decay, freak windstorms blew the perfectly formed shingles upon the wooden walls to form the roof. Then another few billion years passed, and iron from rock and glass from sand were made from the overly heated Earth's core or freak volcanic activity. Mudslides brought them into their present location within the house's structure.

Wouldn't you just shake your head in disbelief if someone actually tried to convince you of such a series of events? My analogy is imperfect, but it's almost certainly more statistically possible than what mathematicians calculate the odds are that our universe came together by random forces. This is why the design argument for the existence of God is so strong.

Patrick Glynn, Harvard Doctoral graduate and former avowed atheist, came to theism and Christianity by the overwhelming evidence of the fine-tuning of the universe as the handiwork of a master craftsman. In his book, *God: The Evidence*, he writes:

> *Gradually, I realized that in the twenty years since I opted for atheism, a vast, systematic literature had emerged that not only cast deep doubt on, but also, from my reasonable perspective, effectively refuted my atheistic outlook. Today, it seems to me, there is no good reason for an intelligent person to embrace the illusion of atheism or agnosticism. Today the concrete data points strongly in the direction of the God hypothesis. It is the simplest and most obvious solution to the puzzle.* [11]

Of course, there are those who still reject the design argument and have come up with other theories for the existence of the universe apart from supernatural design. In the next chapter, we'll briefly explore the two most common arguments against theistic design.

QUESTION 3 *(continued)*

Why is There Order and Not Chaos?

Chapter 6

Explanations of Design

Just The Way It Is

I call the first argument against design the "Just The Way It Is!" argument. This is known in scientific circles as the "Brute Facts" argument. The "Brute Facts" argument goes something like this:

> *All the values of the many forces that have come together to produce life on Earth are simply the brute facts of our existence. The only way we are able to even observe or question them is because they have happened to produce us.*

In other words, our existence is simply "just the way it is." There is no need to try to look for some supernatural design behind it and the only way we can see the brute facts is because we just happen to be here. What a circular argument.

To argue against this response, consider the following "firing-squad" analogy from Oxford educated philosopher John Leslie. As Leslie points out:

> *If fifty sharp shooters draw aim on me and when told to "fire" they all miss me, the response "If they had not missed me I wouldn't be here to consider the fact" is not an adequate answer for my continued existence. I would be curious to know how 50 trained marksmen all "happened" to miss me by "chance." A more reasonable conclusion is there was a premeditated plan to miss. Why would I conclude this? My continued existence would be very improbable under the hypothesis that they missed me by chance, but not improbable under the hypothesis that there was some reason why they missed me.* [1]

Just the fact that I'm here and able to ask the question, "Why am I alive?" isn't enough to negate the evidence of design. Actually, it strengthens it. Some would have you believe that simply beating the odds is enough to prove that the odds can be beaten. A more reasonable approach is to ask how such astronomical odds were beaten.

Would you really accept this argument in a real world setting? For example, what if your next-door neighbor won the lottery jackpot? The odds for winning a multi-state lottery jackpot are roughly 18 million to one. Written in scientific notation, that is 1.8×10^9. Now remember, those odds are far less than any of the numerous forces that need to come together precisely for life on Earth to occur. So, your neighbor won $50 million in such a jackpot. You are amazed at his good fortune to beat the odds (and odds are you're nicer to him than before). Now imagine the very next month, he wins the jackpot again. You're stunned! What would you think if he wins the jackpot for 100 straight months? At what point do you stop believing this is chance and start believing that the lottery is rigged in his favor? If you're a gracious person, you might give him the second win by chance, but by the third straight win, even the most generous person would question the integrity of the system. No reasonable person is going to believe their neighbor can win 100 straight lottery drawings. Imagine you ask your neighbor how he did it and he gives you the "brute facts" argument. He says, "That's just the way it is. We just happen to live in a universe where a person can beat incredible odds 100 straight times. Just be happy for me." C'mon! Really? Do you actually go away satisfied with his answer? Of course you don't. But that's the answer the "Brute Facts" proponents want us to believe.

Paul Davies, in his book, ***The Mind of God***, says,

> *"I cannot believe that our existence in this universe is a mere quirk of fate, an accident of history, an incidental blip in the great cosmic drama. Through my scientific work, I have come to believe more and more strongly that the physical universe is put together with an ingenuity that is so astonishing that I cannot accept it as a brute fact."* [2]

Most realize the "Brute Facts" argument lacks reason and common sense, so a more popular argument has risen. Let's look at the Multi-verse Hypothesis.

Multi-Verse Hypothesis (MVH)

The proponents of the MVH realize that the odds of our universe coming together in such finely tuned precision are ridiculously large. It's beyond reason to believe they could do so given one and only one chance. So, to beat those odds, they propose that there isn't a *uni*verse, but there are many, many universes—*multi*verses. They suggest that we live in one of the almost infinite number of universes. Their reasoning makes sense. If you increase the number of universes, you increase the likelihood that one will fit the parameters that will produce life. Back to our lottery-winning neighbor. If, instead of purchasing one ticket per lottery drawing, he purchases hundreds, even thousands, maybe millions, then he greatly increases his chances of winning. The MVH proponents suggest there is a universe-generating mechanism that we haven't yet discovered that is continually producing universes with all kinds of different properties and laws and values, and we happened to hit the jackpot and wind up in the one that's able to produce life. It sounds reasonable, right? Not so fast. There are several serious flaws with the MVH argument. Let's look at them one at a time.

No Evidence

The first problem — and it is a serious one — for the MVH argument is that there is no physical scientific evidence to give it any credibility. When I say no evidence, what I really mean is no evidence. None. Zip. Nada. Not a shred. Not a clue. Nothing. I have to say I'm always curious about "scientists" and their followers who will propose a viewpoint that has zero scientific credibility. This isn't real science at all. It is faith. It is a metaphysical construct. Here's something I have picked up on when reading all these articles and debates. When a scientist or philosopher or educated debater uses the term "metaphysical," you can just substitute the word "imaginary." That's all it means. Having no evidence isn't the only problem for the MVH argument. Even if we grant that it is a metaphysical possibility, it still has serious problems.

"Metaphysical possibility" is just a fancy term for make-believe. There is nothing wrong with having theories, but if it's not observable or repeatable, then it is no longer true science.

Again, physicist Paul Davies states the atheist's dilemma. "One may find it easier to believe in an infinite array of universes than in an infinite Deity, but such a belief must rest on faith rather than observation."[3] Belief without observation is exactly what atheists accuse theists of doing. It's ironic to see atheists resort to "blind faith."

Universe Generator

For the MVH theory to work, there has to be some sort of universe-generator out there, which we have yet to discover, that is spitting out all these universes, for which there is not a shred of evidence. What exactly would such a generator look like? The most popular view is that of a foaming "sea" of energy that randomly generates these explosive "bubbles" in the form of universes. We just happen to be in one of those universes. Now you're probably asking yourself the same question I asked when I read about this theory, "Where did the generator come from?" An answer to that question wouldn't solve the problem at all. It would just move it up a level. In fact, let's pretend for a moment there is a universe generator out there that is capable of producing finely tuned universes. Wouldn't that generator itself then have to be finely tuned? It violates the law of entropy to suggest that precise order can come from absolute chaos. So if the generator is well designed enough to produce well-ordered universes, or at least one well-ordered universe, then that design has to be explained, doesn't it?

In my opinion, the MVH theory is so far-fetched that it really goes to show the strength of the design hypothesis. Such an outlandish argument demonstrates how far some are willing to go to avoid the thought of theistic design. As journalist, philosopher, and blogger Gregg Easterbrook put it, "The multiverse idea rests on assumptions that would be laughed out of town if they came from a religious text. The theory requires as much suspension of disbelief as any religion. "Join the church that believes in the existence of invisible objects fifty billion galaxies wide." [4]

Dr. William Craig, a research professor of philosophy at Wheaton, states, "There is no real reason to believe that such parallel worlds exist. The very fact that skeptics have come up with such an outlandish theory is because the fine-tuning of the universe points powerfully toward an Intelligent Designer and some people will hypothesize anything to avoid reaching that conclusion." [5]

But some might shout here, "Wait a second! You have a double standard!"

A Double Standard?

The proponents of the MVH argument often assert, "How can you propose a metaphysical supernatural creator that you have never seen while we can't propose a metaphysical multi-verse generator that we can't see?" At first glance, this seems like a legitimate argument, but we will quickly see that it is not. The reason for this is the Principle of Extrapolation. Extrapolation is simply to apply to the unknown future the patterns and trends we see and know in the present. We use the law of extrapolation every day in many ways.

> *Extrapolation: to project, extend, or expand known data or experience into an area not known or experienced so as to arrive at a knowledge of the unknown area.*
> Merriam-Webster

A meteorologist can forecast tomorrow's weather by looking at current weather patterns and radar information and extrapolate what tomorrow will probably look like.

A doctor can listen to a cough, take a temperature, look at x-rays or blood samples, and extrapolate an illness based on the trends and patterns and experiences she has seen in the past.

I can look at my child's messy room and extrapolate based on past trends that the room didn't get that way all by itself. Experience tells me that the teenager was responsible.

When you and I came upon that stone structure in the middle of the New Mexican wilderness, we were certain, based on our past experiences with rocks and wood and living quarters, that the home did not get there by chance, but by intelligent design. This is extrapolation.

Extrapolation is not always correct. The weatherman is sometimes wrong. The doctor doesn't always diagnose accurately, and it may have been my son's friends who tore up his room. Extrapolation isn't one hundred percent accurate, but it does lead us toward what is most probable.

Our Universe is highly and finely tuned to be able to produce life on this planet. This is beyond debate. From what we know about highly and finely tuned mechanisms, we can extrapolate that an intelligent mind is behind it. We don't need to imagine unbeatable odds or wildly creative hypotheses since we have known trends and patterns.

Robin Collins, a leading proponent of the Intelligent Design argument, puts it this way…

> *The first reason for rejecting the atheistic many-universes hypothesis, and preferring the theistic hypothesis, is the following general rule: everything else being equal, we should prefer hypotheses for which we have independent evidence or that are natural extrapolations from what we already know. Let's first illustrate and support this principle, and then apply it to the case of the fine-tuning.*
>
> *Most of us take the existence of dinosaur bones to count as very strong evidence that dinosaurs existed in the past. But suppose a dinosaur skeptic claimed that she could explain the bones by postulating a "dinosaur-bone-producing-field" that simply materialized the bones out of thin air. Moreover, suppose further that, to avoid objections such as that there are no known physical laws that would allow for such a mechanism, the dinosaur skeptic simply postulated that we have not yet discovered these laws or detected these fields. Surely, none of us would let this skeptical hypothesis deter us from inferring the existence of dinosaurs. Why? Because although no one has directly observed dinosaurs, we do have experience of other animals leaving*

> *behind fossilized remains, and thus the dinosaur explanation is a natural extrapolation from our common experience. In contrast, to explain the dinosaur bones, the dinosaur skeptic has invented a set of physical laws, and a set of mechanisms that are not a natural extrapolation from anything we know or experience. In the case of the fine-tuning, we already know that minds often produce fine-tuned devices, such as Swiss watches. Postulating God—a super-mind—as the explanation of the fine-tuning, therefore, is a natural extrapolation from what we already observe minds to do. In contrast, it is difficult to see how the atheistic many-universes hypothesis could be considered a natural extrapolation from what we observe.* [6]

A well-ordered and finely tuned universe doesn't necessarily prove the existence of a supernatural creator. That's not my goal. My goal is to assert that a well-ordered and finely tuned universe is far more likely under a theistic design model than under a model of pure chance or imaginary theories. My deductive argument might look like this.

A. Designed things have a designer
B. The Universe is very well designed
C. The Universe most likely has a designer

Many former skeptics are coming to a theistic worldview based on the overwhelming scientific evidence of design. As Physicist Walter Bradley stated, "It's quite easy to understand why so many scientists have changed their minds in the last thirty years, agreeing that the universe cannot reasonably be explained as a cosmic accident. Evidence for an intelligent designer becomes more compelling the more we understand about our carefully crafted habitat." [7]

I leave it up to theism opponents to produce well designed things that they can prove came about by chance.

"Who Designed God?"

This is one of the last objections skeptics raise when facing the enormous scientific evidence in favor of theistic design. The thinking behind it can be summed up with the words of atheist George Smith. He states, "If the universe is wonderfully designed, surely God is even more wonderfully designed. He must, therefore, have had a designer even more wonderful than He is. If God did not require a designer, then there is no reason why such a relatively less wonderful thing as the universe needed one." [8]

This is really just an elementary school level attempt to avoid the real question and often comes as a last ditch attempt to avoid the implications of design. The question, "Who designed God?" assumes we need to understand or be able to explain the designer if we are going to accept the probability of design. Why make such an assumption? There are innumerable items we see and use on a regular basis that we know are designed, but have no idea of how they were designed or who designed them. Let's return once again to the rock home we found in the New Mexican mountains. Do I really need to know or be able to describe who built the home to come to a conclusion of intelligent design? To suggest that the home wasn't built by design simply because I never met the designers is silly. We can easily infer design from experience and extrapolation without having to know anything about the origin of the designer.

The Grand Designer

John Leslie in *Universes* states that the fine-tuning of the universe is "genuine evidence that God is real." [9] In their book *The New Story of Science,* Augros and Stanciu talk about the amazing organization of many forces that have precisely come together to bring about life. "A universe aiming at the production of man implies a mind directing it. Though man is not at the physical center of the universe, he appears to be at the center of its purpose." [10]

With the first three questions in mind and considering both the Cosmological and Teleological Arguments for the existence of God, what does our universe reveal to us about this creator?

The answers to the second question — just the mere existence of the universe — reveal the Creator to be:

> **Powerful** — this is obvious from the size and scope of the universe — which came from nothing.
>
> **Spaceless** — because it created space, the supernatural cause must exist outside of space.
>
> **Timeless** — because it created time, the supernatural cause must exist outside of time.
>
> **Independent of creation** — this is based on logic and reason. The creator cannot be part of creation that came from nothing. The

creator must be outside of and independent of that creation.

Personal—to change a state of absolute nothingness into something requires volition, and volition is a choice. Choices are made by intelligent beings, not by random forces.

Given the evidence from order we can also add:

Intelligent — The remarkable design of the universe requires a super intelligent being to conceive and construct it. We are clearly talking about a being and not an impersonal force.

Purposed — The well-designed universe isn't just here; it appears designed to produce intelligent life. It has purpose, and that stems from a purposeful Designer.

Section Summary

1. There are two basic arguments for order—pure chance and a designer. Using an old homestead as an illustration, we discussed which seems more reasonable.

2. The universe is remarkably fine-tuned. We briefly discussed just five of the roughly 122 physical laws or forces that have to precisely come together for life to occur.

3. There are two chief arguments against the design hypothesis. We looked at the "brute facts" argument and the "multi-verse hypothesis" as well as weaknesses of each.

4. The *Principle of Extrapolation* gives us far more confidence in choosing the hypothesis of an intelligent designer over some wild theory for which we have no experience or evidence.

5. We concluded the chapter by discussing what the *design* of the universe reveals to us about the *designer* of the universe.

Tough Question 4

Why is There Life?

CHAPTER 7

For ever since the world was created, people have seen the earth and sky. Through everything God made, they can clearly see his invisible qualities—his eternal power and divine nature. So they have no excuse for not knowing God. Romans 1:20

"Ignorance more frequently begets confidence than does knowledge: it is those who know little, not those who know much, who so positively assert that this or that problem will never be solved by science."

CHARLES DARWIN

THUNDER BOOMS AND SHAKES THE castle walls. Flashes of lightning briefly light up the dark night sky. The assistant is feverishly working levers and knobs as the mad scientist paces the floor beside his lifeless experiment. Finally, a perfectly placed lightning bolt strikes the rod. As energy surges into the machine and is conducted to the dead body lying on the table, the creator cries out, "Live! *Live*! *Live*!" The body twitches and moves and finally rises as the scientist, Victor Frankenstein, looks with wonder and fear upon the monster he has created. This is one of the many variations of Mary Shelley's classic. In her original work, the creature was introspective and thoughtful. In other works, he can barely grunt, much less speak. In my personal favorite movie variation, Mel Brooks has young Frankenstein dancing in a tuxedo and top hat while singing, "Putting on the Ritz." The one commonality among all the Frankenstein interpretations is that non-living parts can be stitched together and then brought to life. Life! Not all that difficult. Add a few wires, some electricity and shazam—up and walking around. Easy, right?

This is similar to the same formula for the beginning of life I was taught in ninth grade biology. My high school biology class was taught by Coach Z. We all called him Z for short because we couldn't pronounce his last name. He was a throw-back. In 1979, Coach Z was in his mid-to late-forties, with a missing leg and thinning hair, which he kept in a ponytail. He was passionate about two things: football and biology. He was fun and charismatic and engaging. I looked forward to his class. We dissected frogs, memorized the formula for photosynthesis, and studied the cellular structure of plants as well as the origin of life. Evolutionary science dominated biology textbooks and I bought into all of it. It made a lot of sense to me at the time. In the primordial goo of early Earth, some protein molecules were somehow formed. Add a well-timed lightning strike or two from the hostile environment and presto, you have a single-celled life form. Easy. Early life changed gradually, over time, through the process of mutation and natural selection. Those mutations that worked were passed on and those that didn't were killed off. Toss in a few million years of survival of the fittest, and presto! Looking back at it now, I don't understand how I swallowed it all. I mean, really? Seriously? Are we really going to believe that this thing called life is the product of random chance and

Point to Ponder

If we can't create even the simplest single-celled living organism, with all our intelligence and equipment, in a controlled lab, how do we think it came about by chance under such harsh chaotic conditions as early Earth?

impersonal chaotic forces? Can a living thing really come from natural forces acting upon non-living chemicals? This seems even much more implausible than the stone homestead coming together from random natural events. It begs the question, "Why is there life?" In the previous section, we learned that the Earth is remarkably positioned inside a finely tuned universe with just the right parameters to be able to support life. We still must ask how life came about in the first place. Was Darwin right? Or is there another, more reasonable, explanation? In Tough Question Two, we looked at the cosmological evidence of creation for the existence of a Creator. In Tough Question Three, we looked at the teleological evidence of design that points to a designer. Now we will look at the biological evidence that leads us to a life giver. Let's first turn our attention to some of the most crucial elements of evolutionary theory.

TOUGH QUESTION 4 *(continued)*

Why is There Life?

Chapter 8

Natural Explanations

In the Beginning

Before life can "evolve," it has to begin. For evolution to work, there has to be a living thing for it to work on, and that's a problem for those who hold to evolution as the origin of life. It is very difficult to have a scientific theory without having the observable and reproducible mechanisms to support that theory. Those elements are the basis of real science, and they are seriously lacking here. We, with all our laboratories, intelligence, and technology, have not been able to even come close to reproducing the conditions needed for life to occur. If we can't do it with all our collective intelligence, how can we really believe that it happened by chance? And yet, even without this crucial beginning, evolutionary theory goes on. It's like a fairy tale: "Once upon a time, there was primitive life. Then, evolutionary processes took over, and poof. Here we are. And we all lived happily ever after." Without being able to provide scientific evidence for the beginning of life, evolution really has no foundation upon which to stand. Of course, there have been attempts. The most famous of these attempts to show how life began are Stanley Miller's experiments in the early 1950's. These are the ones I learned about in Coach Z's class (and I was told they worked). Let's look at the Miller experiments.

The Miller Experiments

The Miller, or Miller–Urey, experiments were a series of experiments conducted by Stanley Miller and Harold Urey in 1952 and then published in 1953 at the University of Chicago. The purpose of these experiments was to simulate early Earth conditions and create organic compounds (amino acids) from inorganic material. Amino acids are the basic building blocks of proteins, which form the basis for life. The goal was to show that amino acids could come from purely natural conditions and then lead to life itself. Using Water, Ammonia, Methane and Hydrogen (elements thought at the time to form the Earth's early atmosphere) a spark was applied (simulating lighting) and at the end of a week they discovered that several amino acids had formed. (see graphic)

The experiment was hailed as a huge success, and scientists began formulating theories about how those amino acids later formed into complex chains of proteins and how those complex chains eventually formed life. A wave of euphoria swept the scientific community. They believed the mechanism for life was found. More articles were written and high school textbooks, including mine, contained the experiment as part of the teaching on evolution. Sixty years later, the Miller experiment has come under much scrutiny and is rejected by most of the scientific community. It has many problems.

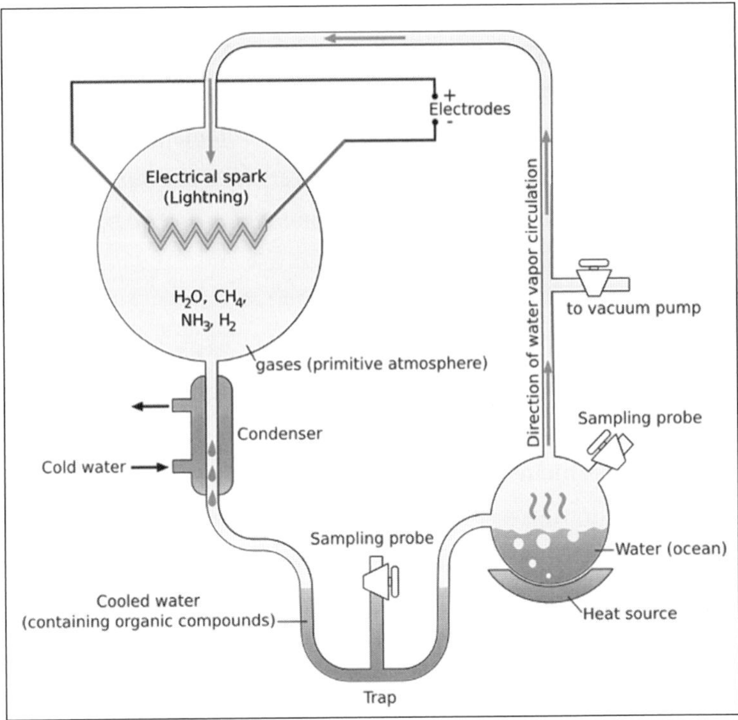

Wrong Atmosphere

In the last several decades, scientists have learned that the "atmosphere" Miller and Urey used in their experiment was nowhere close to what conditions on early Earth were like. By the 1980's, scientists agreed that Nitrogen and Carbon Dioxide should have been used instead of Methane and Ammonia. As Kevin McKean wrote in Discover magazine,

> *"Miller and Urey imitated the ancient atmosphere on the Earth with a mixture of methane and ammonia. However, in the latest studies, it has been understood that the Earth was very hot at those times, and that*

> *it was composed of melted nickel and iron. Therefore, the chemical atmosphere of that time should have been formed mostly of nitrogen (N_2), carbon dioxide (CO_2), and water vapor (H_2O). However, these are not as appropriate as methane and ammonia for the production of organic molecules."* [1]

Why did Miller and Urey use the other gasses? Precisely because they knew they would help in the formation of amino acids. The American scientists J. P. Ferris and C. T. Chen repeated Miller's experiment with an atmospheric environment that contained carbon dioxide, hydrogen, nitrogen, and water vapor, and were unable to obtain even a single amino acid molecule.[2] A wrong atmosphere is not the only problem with the experiment.

Wrong Environment

In his earlier experiments, Miller noticed the amino acids that were created were immediately destroyed by the surrounding environment—namely the sparking mechanism. So, in his "successful" experiment, he created a "cold trap" that isolated the newly formed amino acids away from the spark. This safe zone allowed the acids to continue to exist. What's wrong with that? Well, if your goal is to form amino acids, then nothing is wrong with it. However, if your goal is to show how organic compounds could have been formed in the harsh environment of early Earth by natural processes, then this "safety zone" is completely unrealistic. As chemist Richard Bliss states, "Actually, without this trap, the chemical products would have been destroyed by the energy source."[3]

Today, the vast majority of scientists regard the Miller-Urey experiment as completely inadequate to explain how life originated on Earth. Even the evolutionist publication *Earth* admits this. In the February 1998 issue, the following statements appear in an article titled "Life's Crucible":

> *"Geologists now think that the primordial atmosphere consisted mainly of carbon dioxide and nitrogen, gases that are less reactive than those used in the 1953 experiment. And even if Miller's atmosphere could have existed, how do you get simple molecules, such as amino acids, to go through the necessary chemical changes that will convert them into more complicated compounds, or polymers, such as proteins? Miller himself throws up his hands at that part of the puzzle. "It's a problem," he sighs with exasperation. "How do you make polymers? That's not so easy."*[4]

Why is it so important to look closely at this? Neither the Miller experiment nor any subsequent experiment in the last sixty years has even come close to explaining how life on Earth began. This is a serious problem if one is going to embrace the worldview that life happened by random, natural forces. All of the research shows that it's unreasonable to believe that life emerged by chance. The alternative view is that life was created. The reason evolutionists do not accept this obvious option is their blind adherence to prejudices that are totally unscientific. Harold Urey, Miller's professor and assistant on the 1952 experiment, made the following admission:

> *"All of us who study the origin of life find that the more we look into it, the more we feel it is too complex to have evolved anywhere. We all believe as an article of faith that life evolved from dead matter on this planet. It is just that its complexity is so great, it is hard for us to imagine that it did."* [5]

"Article of faith?" That doesn't belong in science, does it? As we continue to look at the naturalist's worldview, we will see an astonishing amount of blind faith. Regardless of the lack of any evidence or ability to reproduce the origin of life, many still embrace, by faith, that evolution is the mechanism that brought about life on Earth. Let's review the basic premises of evolutionary belief and then see if it is the most reasonable belief for explaining life as we know it.

Evolution – An Overview

Charles Darwin was born the fifth of six children in February of 1809. Blessed to be born into wealthy society, and raised in the Anglican Church, he showed a love for natural history and collection by age eight. By age sixteen, he was an apprentice doctor to his father, Robert. He decided not to go into the field of medicine, which upset his father, but became more and more fascinated with naturalism. In late 1931, at the age of twenty-two, Charles was invited to travel as a self-funded observer/collector aboard the HMS Beagle. He joined Captain Robert Fitzroy and crew on a two-year journey to chart the coastline of South America. On December 27th, 1831, Darwin boarded the Beagle and the ensuing *five*-year sailing trip led to one of the most influential writings in human history.

Over the course of those five years, Darwin visited many countries and islands. He studied rock formations in Chile and found seashells in the Andes. In Australia, he came across the strange kangaroo rat and humorously wrote that "two different creators" made the platypus. In the Galapagos Islands, he was struck by the difference in the beaks of Finches, depending upon their particular environment. Darwin compiled a large collection and took copious notes, many of which he forwarded to England. By the time he returned to England on October 2, 1836, Darwin was already somewhat of a celebrity. Over the next three years, he continued to refine his ideas on natural selection, a term he preferred over evolution. In November 1839 he published, ***On the Origin of Species***. His goal was to help explain how natural forces, such as mutation, natural selection, and survival of the fittest, would help "throw light on the origin of man and his history." [6]

His theory is stated simply in his introduction:

> *"As many more individuals of each species are born than can possibly survive; and as, consequently, there is a frequently recurring struggle for existence, it follows that any being, if it vary however slightly in any manner profitable to itself, under the complex and sometimes varying conditions of life, will have a better chance of surviving, and thus be naturally selected. From the strong principle of inheritance, any selected variety will tend to propagate its new and modified form."* [7]

By the 1870's, Darwinian evolution was considered the scientific explanation for both the origin and variety of life on Earth. Over one hundred years later this theory is taught in schools as *the* explanation for life. It's what I learned from Coach Z over thirty years ago. Let's review the basics of this theory.

Mutation

Evolution depends on mutations, or genetic variations. Slight changes in the genetic code produce offspring that are not exact copies of their parents. A slightly larger wing, a longer beak, darker skin, or any one of millions of genetic options. The widespread belief in mutation as the engine that drives evolution extends far past the classroom and into popular culture.

My family and I are big fans of the X-men movies. As a young boy, I spent many hours reading the X-men comics. The theme of mutation and evolution is the entire premise of the storyline. Just this week, we watched X-Men First Class and several times, the brilliant scientist and future leader of the X-Men, Charles Xavier, states, "Mutation is how we went from a single-celled organism to the dominant species on Earth." The offspring, genetically different from its parents, is born into the harsh world and the next force, Natural Selection, takes over.

In "X-Men: First Class," that line on genetics was his pick-up line for the ladies in bars.

Natural Selection

Natural selection, often called Survival of the Fittest, is simply the natural weeding-out of traits that are less than desirable.

This natural selection process assures that the strongest, fastest, best equipped offspring will survive to reproduce and carry on the species.

So far, neither of these processes is shocking. We see both of them happen in nature all the time. There are many varieties of dogs, cats, etc. We see humans with many different skin colors and heights and other variations. Natural selection happens on a regular basis as well. A pride of lions stalking a herd of wildebeest will identify the weak, the slow, and the injured. They "deselect" them from breeding, thus leaving the stronger, faster, and more equipped to carry on their genes.

Both of these natural forces are observable and reproducible, thus making them very scientific. It's the next leap that puts Darwinian evolution on very shaky ground. The term used is Transmutation of species.

Transmutation of Species

We can observe mutation and natural selection occur *within* a species on a regular basis. This helps species adapt to a changing environment. This is called "Micro" evolution. Darwin noted this evolution in the beaks of Finches in the Galapagos Islands and how they varied with their surroundings. Finches' beaks may change according to the terrain and available food, but they are still finches. Longer-necked giraffes survive because they can reach higher into trees for food, but they are still giraffes. Within a species genetic boundary, there is room for variation and change, but there is no evidence for a species crossing that boundary and becoming another species. I personally believe the term "micro-evolution" is a misnomer and used to help "sell" the larger belief system of evolution. What is termed "micro-evolution" is really nothing more than variation within genetic limitations for a species.

However, when most use the term "evolution," they are referring to "Macro" evolution. This view suggests that what happens within a species is also the mechanism for actually creating new species. That's where we get the term "Transmutation of Species." Fish eventually mutate into amphibians, which then later lead to reptiles, then onto birds and mammals, and finally, you.

This follows the principle of extrapolation we discussed. If we see evolution within a species, can't we then extrapolate that process and suggest that is how *all* the species came to be? That's the basic premise of Darwin's book and all of evolutionary theory since. I have no problem with presenting a possible theory and then testing to see if it works. That's what real science does.

But does the evidence support the theory? Is this the most reasonable conclusion for life as we know it? While genetic variation and micro-evolution have been observed, it cannot be used as evidence for macro-evolution, which has not been observed. In other words, natural selection may account for the *survival* of a species, but it cannot account for the *arrival* of a species. Let's examine the evidence next.

Natural selection may account for the survival of a species, but it cannot account for the arrival of a species.

THE FOSSIL RECORD

As Charles Darwin (and Charles Xavier) stated, evolution asserts that all of life stemmed from a single source in the distant past. Over millions of years and countless mutations and variations, life branched off into the many species we see today. If this were true, then the fossil record would clearly show this long, transitional story of life. We would come across myriads of strange and exciting creatures that were "deselected" by nature. We would not need to look for "missing links." There should be millions, even billions, of fossilized creatures that show the long history of variation and arrival of new forms. Darwin himself knew this is what was needed:

> *"If my theory be true, numberless intermediate varieties, linking most closely all of the species of the same group together must assuredly have existed...Consequently, evidence of their former existence could be found only amongst fossil remains."* [8]

Unfortunately for those who hold to evolutionary theory, the fossil record does not show this at all. Over one hundred years ago, Darwin himself was very aware that the fossil record did not support his theory:

> *"Why, if species have descended from other species by fine gradations, do we not everywhere see innumerable transitional forms? Why is not all nature in confusion, instead of the species being, as we see them, well defined? But, as by this theory innumerable transitional forms must have existed, why do we not find them embedded*

> *in countless numbers in the crust of the Earth? But in the intermediate region, having intermediate conditions of life, why do we not now find closely linking intermediate varieties? This difficulty for a long time quite confounded me."* [9]

He hoped that further fossil discoveries would support his theory. However, today, like Darwin, evolutionists are still confounded by enormous "gaps" in the fossil record. In the 170 years since *Origin of the Species* was published, paleontologists have discovered literally billions of fossils. The fossil record is rich. However, despite the abundance of fossil sources, not a single transitional form has been uncovered, and it's unlikely that any transitional forms will be found as a result of new excavations. Many prominent scientists agree. A professor of paleontology from Glasgow University, T. Neville George, admitted this fact years ago:

> *"There is no need to apologize any longer for the poverty of the fossil record. In some ways, it has become almost unmanageably rich and discovery is outpacing integration.The fossil record nevertheless continues to be composed mainly of gaps."* [10]

And Niles Eldredge, the well-known paleontologist and curator of the American Museum of Natural History, expresses the invalidity of Darwin's claim that the insufficiency of the fossil record is the reason why no transitional forms have been found:

> *"The record jumps, and all the evidence shows that the record is real: the gaps we see reflect real events in life's history — not the artifact of a poor fossil record."* [11]

This is the elephant in the middle of the room for evolutionists. The evidence for evolution simply does not exist. It should be there. It should be easy to find. But it's not there. Life did not come about in one long, slow process of variation and selection. It appears not gradually, but more like an explosion. In fact, that's the name given to the brief window of time in which we see most of life emerge on Earth: the Cambrian Explosion.

> *If evolution were true, then the fossil record would be filled with an innumerable variety of species showing the long, gradual change of life. It simply isn't there.*

The Cambrian Explosion

Sometimes called biology's "Big Bang," the Cambrian explosion is a very difficult obstacle for those wanting to hold onto an evolutionary origin of life. Remember, evolution predicts a long, slow, gradual change of species. That should be seen in the fossil record. But the Cambrian explosion shows us just the opposite. Beginning about 540 million years ago, in a very brief amount of time, geologically speaking, every major skeletal type we know of today burst onto the scene with no predecessors to descend from. This is huge! It also violates everything that evolutionary theory predicts. Contrary to the "tree of life" that many of us were taught as depicting the evolutionary pattern, the actual evidence shows us something much different. We see a 450-million-year-old fossilized horseshoe crab that looks

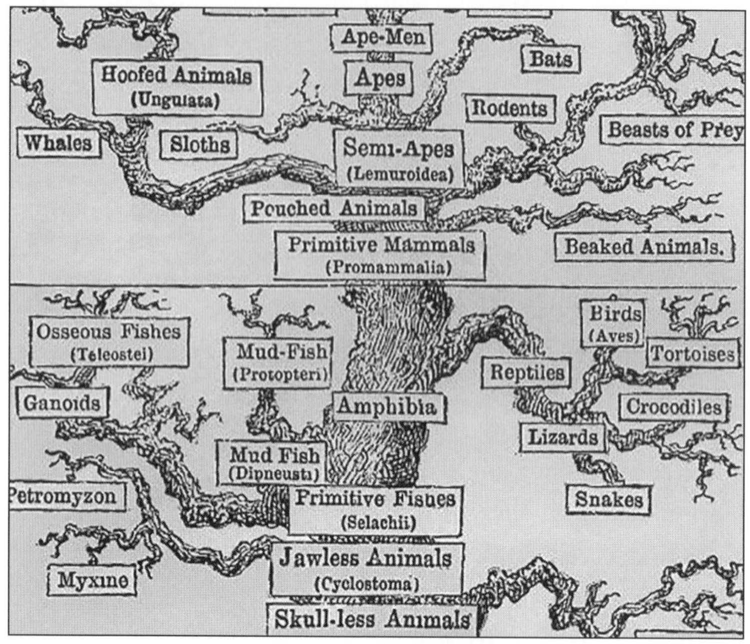

Darwin's Tree of Life

exactly like a modern one. 400-million-year-old oysters are just like ones you find today. A 140-million-year-old dragonfly found in Bavaria, Germany is indistinguishable from one flying around by your local lake. A 170-million-year-old shrimp looks exactly like the one I ate just last night on a date with my wife.

This "explosion" of life with no preceding generations is an enormous obstacle for evolutionists. Many world-class scientists agree.

Stephen Gould, writing for *Discover* magazine, states,

> *"The most famous such burst, the Cambrian explosion, marks the inception of modern multicellular life. Within just a few million years, nearly every major kind of animal anatomy appears in the fossil record for the first*

time. The Precambrian record is now sufficiently good that the old rationale about undiscovered sequences of smoothly transitional forms will no longer wash." [12]

Even Richard Dawkins, one of the most influential atheists alive today, has to concede this evidence, or lack thereof:

"And we find many of them [Cambrian fossils] already in an advanced state of evolution, the very first time they appear. It is as though they were just planted there, without any evolutionary history. Needless to say, this appearance of sudden planting has delighted creationists." [13]

Mr. Dawkins misses the point. It shouldn't be whether the evidence delights or disturbs anyone. The main question is, what does the evidence say? The evidence from the fossil record simply says that evolution is not true. Sadly, in an attempt to keep the failing belief system of evolution alive, there have been many frauds, followed by an ensuing rush to judgment, perpetuated on the public.

The "Piltdown Man" Hoax

Hailed as one of the most important transitional discoveries in history, the "Piltdown Man" find was an instant worldwide story. A jawbone, teeth, and some tools were discovered in 1912 by an amateur paleontologist and well known doctor, Charles Dawson, in a pit near Piltdown, England. While visiting the British Museum in 1921, leading American paleontologist Henry Fairfield Osborn said, "We have to be reminded over and over

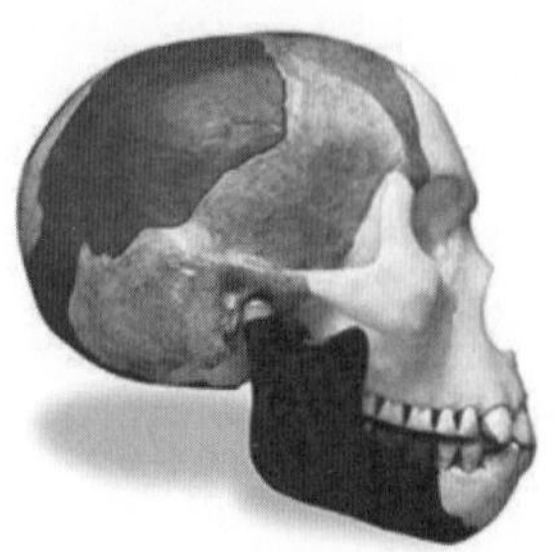

Artist's Rendering of the Piltdown Man

again that Nature is full of paradoxes," and proclaimed Piltdown, "a discovery of transcendent importance to the prehistory of man." [14]

Alleged to be 500,000 years old, the remains were displayed in several museums as absolute proof of human evolution. For more than 40 years, many scientific articles were written on "Piltdown Man," many interpretations and drawings were made, and the fossil was presented as important evidence for human evolution. No fewer than 500 doctoral theses were written on the subject.

However, in 1949, the truth came to light. Kenneth Oakley from the British Museum's Paleontology Department did further studies and testing and made a shocking discovery. The teeth in the jawbone, belonging to an orangutan, had been worn down artificially, and the "primitive" tools discovered with the fossils were simple imitations that had been sharpened with steel implements. In the detailed analysis completed by Joseph Weiner, this forgery was revealed to the public in 1953. The skull belonged to a 500-year-old man, and the jawbone belonged to a recently deceased ape! The teeth had been specially arranged in a particular way and added to the jaw, and the molar surfaces were filed in order to resemble those of a man. Then all these pieces were stained with potassium dichromate to give them an old appearance. These stains began to disappear when dipped in acid. Sir Wilfred Le Gros Clark, who was on the team that uncovered the forgery, could not hide his astonishment at this situation, and said, "The evidences of artificial abrasion immediately sprang to the eye. Indeed, so obvious did they seem it may well be asked—how was it that they had escaped notice before?" [15]

The reason the "obvious" had not sprung to the eye is simple. When we are predetermined to believe a certain thing, it doesn't matter what the actual evidence says. We believe what we want to believe. In the wake of all this, "Piltdown Man" was hurriedly removed from the British Museum, where it had been displayed for more than forty years.

Unfortunately, that's not the only hoax perpetuated on a gullible scientific community.

THE "NEBRASKA MAN" HOAX

In 1922, ten years after the Piltdown Man "discovery", another find was made. Across the Atlantic in the state of Nebraska, Henry Fairfield Osborn, the director of the American Museum of Natural History, declared that he had found a fossil molar tooth belonging to the Pliocene period in western Nebraska near Snake Brook. This is the same Henry Osborn who visited the "Piltdown Man" exhibit in England and proclaimed it a transcendent discovery. This tooth allegedly bore common characteristics of both man and ape. An extensive scientific debate began surrounding this fossil, which came to be called "Nebraska Man." Some interpreted this tooth as belonging to Pithecanthropus erectus, while others claimed it was closer to human beings. Nebraska man was also immediately given a "scientific name," *Hesperopithecus*.

Many authorities gave Osborn their support. Based on this single tooth, reconstructions of Nebraska man's head and body were drawn. Moreover, *Hesperopithecus* was even pictured along with his wife and children, as a whole family in a natural setting.

Nebraska Man

Keep in mind that all of these scenarios were developed from just one tooth. Evolutionist circles placed such faith in this "ghost man" that when a researcher named William Bryan opposed these biased conclusions for relying on a single tooth, he was harshly criticized.

Unfortunately for the evolutionary community, more digging was done on the site in 1927, and more of the actual skeleton was found. The tooth of *Hesperopithecus* was actually nothing more than...wait for it...a pig's tooth! William Gregory entitled the article published in *Science,* in which he announced the truth, "Hesperopithecus Apparently Not an Ape Nor a Man."[16] All the drawings of *Hesperopithecus* and his "family" were quickly removed from evolutionary literature and the scientific community said little about it.

While the scams of "Piltdown Man" and "Nebraska Man" were embarrassments to the evolutionary community, they are not the biggest scams. By far the biggest hoax ever played on the public is that of Haeckel's embryos.

Haeckel's Embryos

One of the enduring images of evolutionary teaching is that of the embryonic drawings of German biologist Ernst Heinrich Philipp August Haeckel (1834-1919). To understand the importance of his drawings we must realize that for evolutionary theory to be true the evidence must show common ancestry in the fossil record. We've already shown that the fossil record is void of evidence to support the slow transitions of one species to another. Since this approach was not working and little evidence was being found another approach was tried. It was postulated that our evolutionary transitions could be found in embryonic development.

Does the development of an embryo reveal its evolutionary story? This was the thinking of many and the reason behind Haeckel's drawings. He was a strong supporter of Darwin and wanted to show that embryonic development would reveal evolutionary transitions. He developed his theory of "Recapitulation."

I clearly remember having to memorize the phrase, "Ontogeny Recapitulates Phylogeny" for one of Coach Z's tests. This is the claim that an individual organism's biological development, or ontogeny, parallels and summarizes its species' entire evolutionary development, or phylogeny. To prove this theory, he published his drawings of a variety of embryos to show their similarity at different stages. There were over 100 detailed and colored drawings made from photographs. These drawings have been used in thousands of textbooks to teach millions of children (including myself) and college students the belief of common ancestry. There is just one problem—they're faked!

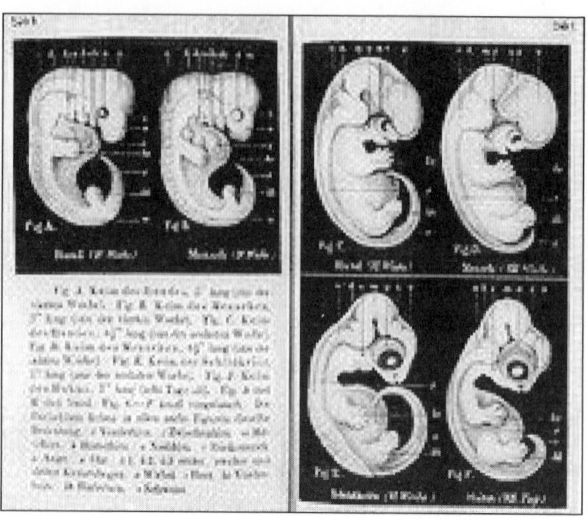

Haeckel's Forged Drawings

Haeckel was so certain of his theory that he manipulated the drawings to show what he believed to be true. Some drawings are doctored. For others, he simply used the same template for different embryos. He mislabeled the timeline of the development of some embryos so they would look more similar in their early stages. In short, he manipulated the evidence to fit the theory. This is not new news. Even his colleagues in 1860 accused him of fraud. Nevertheless, as we have seen in the "Piltdown" and "Nebraska" Man hoaxes, just about anything that will support evolutionary theory is quickly embraced, no matter how absurd. Even though scientists have known for over a century that the drawings are frauds, they are still used in textbooks today. Evolutionist and Harvard professor Stephen Gould admits the misuse of the drawings, calling it, "The academic equivalent of murder." [17]

What does all this mean? The inability to show how life began, the unsupportive fossil record, the hoaxes, the falsified embryonic development. What does it mean? It simply means that evolutionary "science" isn't really science at all. It is a belief system—a faith. Real science is to test that which is observable and reproducible. Evolution is neither. It's a theory with no real evidence, and often manipulated evidence, to support the theory.

We are trying to answer our fourth Tough Question, "Why is There Life?" So far, natural forces can't explain either the beginning of life nor its incredible complexity and variation. Is there another possible explanation? If a creator is the best explanation for the existence of the universe (Tough Question Two), and a creator is the best explanation for the amazing order and design of the universe (Tough Question Three), it stands to reason that a creator might also be a reasonable explanation for life on Earth. But is there any evidence of such a creator? Yes! We will examine those evidences next.

Tough Question 4 *(continued)*

Why is There Life?

Chapter 9

Evidences of Supernatural Creation

The Evidence from Biological Information

In 1953, Francis Crick and James Watson made an astonishing discovery for which they later won the Nobel Prize. It revolutionized the way we look at life — the chemical structure of the DNA molecule. DNA was first discovered in 1869, but its role in genetics was not really known until 1943. A decade later, Crick and Watson discovered the now famous double helix makeup of the DNA molecule, which led to further discoveries of how its coding built the necessary proteins to create life.

In the definitions below, take note of some of the key words (highlighting is mine) used to describe the DNA molecule:

From the Encyclopedia Britannica:

"The linear sequence of nucleotides in DNA contains the *information* for protein sequences."

From Wikipedia:

> "DNA, is a nucleic acid that contains the genetic *instructions,* used in the development, and functioning of all known living organisms. The main role of DNA molecules is the long-term storage of *information.* DNA is often compared to a set of *blueprints,* like a *recipe* or a *code,* since it contains the *instructions* needed to construct other components of cells, such as proteins and RNA molecules."

Notice the words in italics. *Information. Instructions. Blueprints. Recipe. Code.* These are not arbitrarily chosen words, but rather they accurately describe the nature and function of the DNA molecule. The incredibly amazing storage system of the double helix contains all the information necessary to build all the proteins required for the organism to exist. This complex coding system raises a very serious question, however. Have you ever seen information or instructions, codes, a recipe, or a set of blueprints come from anything other than an intelligent source? I would suspect your answer is no.

As George Sim Johnson rightly notes:

> *"Human DNA contains more organized information than the Encyclopedia Britannica. If the full text of the encyclopedia were to arrive in computer code from outer space, most people would regard this as proof of the existence of extraterrestrial intelligence. But when seen in nature, it is explained as the working of random forces."* [1]

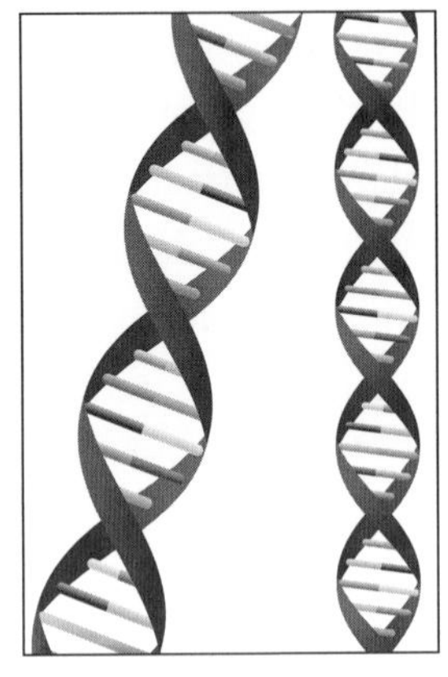

The DNA molecule is a marvel of design and function. Every one of your body's one hundred trillion cells contains a tightly wrapped DNA molecule. Each one of these molecules, if stretched out, would measure approximately six feet in length. These molecules provide the genetic information to create all the different types of proteins that make up you and me. The amount of information DNA stores is mind-boggling. Michael Denton gives us an idea of its incredible capacity:

> *"It vastly exceeds that of any other known system. In fact, the information needed to build the proteins for all the species of organisms that have ever lived — a number estimated to be approximately one thousand million — could be held in a single teaspoon and there would still be room left for all the information in every book ever written."* [2]

That is mind blowing!

Like many of you, I use a computer almost every day. I study, write, research and do many other functions on it. At this very moment, I'm writing this sentence on my home computer. For a computer to work, it has to have a code — a language. This code takes everything the user inputs, like my typing, and puts it into the computer's own language. Every picture, icon, sentence, graphic, and function has, at its core, this computer language, ultimately boiled down to a binary, or two-digit code. As a high school junior and senior, I spent countless hours programming computer code. It was the early 1980's and I was in on the cutting edge of desktop computing. My high school had one of the first computer labs in the area, and I would skip other classes to head down to Mr. Wilkinson's classroom and slip into the lab to do some programming. I wrote an inventory control program for my high school to use to keep track of all its stuff. I wrote a statistics program for our basketball team to use in tracking each player's performances, game by game. The user of each of these programs would simply input the information they wanted stored or tracked and the program I wrote would do the rest. The user didn't have to have any idea of what was going on behind the scenes, as line after line of computer code was simply doing what I, the programmer, had told it to do. Thirty years later, every computer still works this way.

Written language works in the same way. English is a set of twenty-six symbols that, when properly arranged, convey a thought. Those symbols must be arranged in a precise fashion or the language will be useless.

> Esuo nfosi foecnase ntenar lmody alptresced elt.
> A sentence of randomly placed letters is of no use.

The two sentences above have the same exact letters, but the first sentence is complete nonsense due to its randomness.

DNA works in *exactly* the same way as a computer code or written language. It is a chemical code comprised of four bases: Adenine (A), Cytosine (C), Guanine (G), and Thymine (T). This four bit code, A, C, G and T, forms the information language of all of life. But just like computer code or a written language, they can't be put in any random order and work properly. Written in a very specific manner, DNA serves as the information storehouse for a finely choreographed protein manufacturing process.

Everything has to be just right to produce the right bonds in the right sequence to produce the right proteins that fold in the right way to build our body's biological system. That's a whole lot of "right" to happen by accident. To believe that all this ordered code and information and language happened by chaos and random chance is an insult to intelligence.

Would you believe it if I told you that a tornado blew through a print shop to create Hamlet? Of course you wouldn't, and Shakespeare's work is far less complex than a DNA molecule. If we understand that all language and computer code requires an intelligent "writer," it is not a difficult extrapolation to believe an intelligent being wrote the DNA code.

It takes far more faith to believe that such an incredibly well designed information system came about by accident than by an intelligent author.

It is not only the complexity of the code that points to intelligent authorship and away from natural explanations, but also the sequence of events that has to take place for life-building proteins to be created.

DNA can only replicate itself with the help of special enzymes. Those enzymes are created by information stored in the DNA molecule. Do you see the paradox in this process? DNA had to be around to formulate the enzymes, but the enzymes had to be around to reproduce the DNA. This is a great dilemma for naturalists, since evolution demands a slow process of linear progression.

Information systems come from intelligence.

DNA is a biological information system.

DNA must come from intelligence.

Science writer John Horgan explains the dilemma in this way: "DNA cannot do its work, including forming more DNA, without the help of catalytic proteins, or enzymes. In short, proteins cannot form without DNA, but neither can DNA form without proteins."[3]

Dr. Leslie Orgel is a highly renowned naturalist from the University of San Diego, California, and a close associate of Stanley Miller and Francis Crick's. In a 1994 article he says,

> *"It is extremely improbable that proteins and nucleic acids, both of which are structurally complex, arose spontaneously in the same place at the same time. Yet it also seems impossible to have one without the other. And so, at first glance, one might have to conclude that life could never, in fact, have originated by chemical means."*[4]

If life did not originate by natural, chemical means, which we now see is virtually impossible, is it not quite logical and reasonable to assert that it came about by supernatural means?

For many years, Francis Crick believed in the theory of molecular evolution, but eventually even he, the co-discoverer of the DNA molecule, had to admit that such a complex molecule could not have emerged spontaneously, by chance, as the result of an evolutionary process:

> *"An honest man, armed with all the knowledge available to us now, could only state that, in some sense, the origin of life appears, at the moment, to be almost a miracle."*[5]

Evidence continues to mount in favor of supernatural design while problems continue to mount for those who firmly embrace the power of chance. It's increasingly clear that those who embrace evolution and natural forces do so on the power of faith and not that of science. As Australian biologist Michael Denton rightly notes about the faith of the atheist,

> *"To the skeptic, the proposition that the genetic programmes of higher organisms, consisting of something close to a thousand million bits of information, equivalent to the sequence of letters in a small library of 1,000 volumes, containing in encoded form countless thousands of intricate algorithms controlling, specifying, and ordering the growth and development of billions and billions of cells into the form of a complex organism, were composed by a purely random process is simply an affront to reason. But to the Darwinist, the idea is accepted without a ripple of doubt!"* [6]

It is a simple, irrefutable fact: there are no known natural laws that can produce specified complexity like information. Only intelligence has ever created such complexity.

The complexity of biological information on the molecular level is not the only evidence that points to a supernatural creator. Those amazing DNA molecules create astounding proteins which often form together to make manufacturing machines. You read that right, microscopic biological machines. Let's look at those next.

The Evidence from Biological Machines

Imagine walking into a large manufacturing plant and seeing a well-orchestrated system in constant motion. Conveyor belts carry boxes from one part of the plant to another. Forklifts carry and stack inventory in an ordered manner. Engines and motors are built and repaired to keep the process going. All of this activity is going on within the plant while the plant itself is a mobile unit, consistently on the go, moving wherever needed. Any plant manager would love such an efficient, effective, and productive workplace, but none exists, except inside the body. The cell is the most efficient manufacturing plant known to man. Back in Darwin's day, very little was known about the cell. It was just a vague, blotchy mystery. With the advancement of technology, we know it's so much more. As we unlock the mysteries of the cell, we see that it's incredibly complex and filled with microscopic biological machines. I'm not using the word machine as a metaphor or an analogy, but as an accurate description of these microscopic wonders. As Bruce Alberts states in a 1998 edition of *Cell:*

> *"We have always underestimated cells...The entire cell can be viewed as a factory that contains an elaborate network of interlocking assembly lines, each of which is composed of a set of large protein machines...Why do we call the large protein assemblies that underlie cell function protein machines? Precisely because, like machines invented by humans to deal efficiently with the macroscopic world, these protein assemblies contain highly coordinated moving parts."* [7]

If we were to stumble upon such an "elaborate network of interlocking assembly lines" deep in the Amazon Jungle or a remote part of the Sahara Desert, would we not quickly conclude an intelligent source? Why is it any different when we discover these miniature factories deep within our own bodies?

Common Descent or Common Design?

Those who embrace naturalism must believe in the common descent of all living things. They believe, by faith, that all life began with one single cell sparked to life under hostile conditions. Then they believe, by faith, that all of life descended from that common ancestor via countless billions of unseen mutations and selections. But, since they can't find such descent in the fossil record, they often turn to living things and point out obvious similarities. These similarities, they say, point to common ancestry or common descent. However, there is another very common-sense answer to those commonalities.

The following is a transcript of a 1986 debate between evolutionist Paul Kurtz and design proponent Norm Geisler:

> Geisler: Quoting atheist Chandra Wickramasinghe, "believing that life came by chance is like believing that a Boeing 747 resulted from a tornado going through a junk yard." You have to have a lot of faith to believe that!
>
> Kurtz: Well, the Boeing 747 evolved. We can go back to the Wright brothers and see that the first airplane they created…

Geisler: Created?

Kurtz: Yes, but…

Moderator John Ankerberg: By intelligence or by chance?

Kurtz: There was a period of time in which these forms changed.

Ankerberg: But didn't they create those airplanes using intelligence?

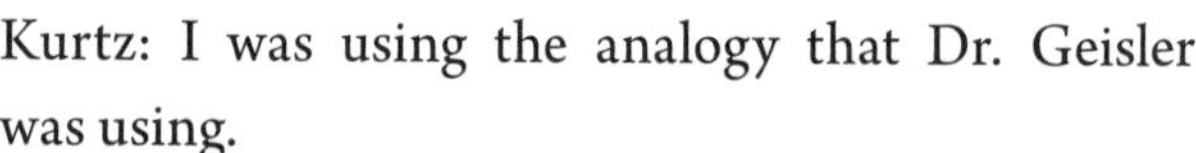

Kurtz: I was using the analogy that Dr. Geisler was using.

Geisler: Well, you're helping my argument! You ought to drop that one and find another one!

Kurtz: No, no, I think the point I make is a good one because there have been changes from the simplest to the more complex airplanes.

Geisler: Yes, but those changes were by intelligent intervention!

I'm personally astounded that Mr. Kurtz could not see the fallacy of his argument. The reason the airplanes have similar traits is not because of blind natural selection, but because of common design powered by intelligence. What is true of airplanes is also true of living things, which are infinitely more complex. Common constructions show common design.

Since we are talking about airplanes, let's take a look at just one example of common design in living things—wings.

Wings and the reality of flight provide a great obstacle for those who reject common design. For evolution to work, random mutations must move to succeeding generations as changes take shape; from swimming creatures, to crawling creatures, to walking creatures, to flying creatures. This agonizingly slow process completely lacks any representation in the fossil record.

Common Descent or Common Design?

According to the theory of evolution, wings emerged independently of each other on four separate occasions: insects, flying reptiles, birds, and flying mammals (bats). The suggestion that wings with very similar structures randomly developed four times—which cannot be explained by the mechanisms of mutation and natural selection—is a very big problem for evolutionary biologists.

The theory of evolved winged flight doesn't just violate the fossil record, it also violates common sense. Think about it — we are supposed to believe an animal that is midway through evolution from a lizard to a bird—half lizard, half bird— is survival of the fittest, right? Picture this miserable creature with me. This Lizbird can no longer run very fast due to its changing bone, muscle, and hip structure. To complicate matters, its only partially developed wings are not yet ready for flight. So here's this hapless animal, trying to escape a predator. It's flapping, but not flying, more waddling than running. Lizbird has no chance. This creature is not the fittest—it's only fit to be a predator's dinner!

If I had any artistic capabilities, I'd love to draw my "lizbird" to show how silly such evolutionary belief really is. Any partially evolved creature would be equally doomed.

What's true of wings is true for many other similarities across species. Here is what Biology teacher Frank Salisbury said about this principle as applied to eyes.

> *"Even something as complex as the eye has appeared several times; for example, in the squid, the vertebrates, and the arthropods. It's bad enough accounting for the origin of such things once, but the thought of producing them several times according to the modern synthetic theory makes my head swim."* [8]

The truth is, *no* directional change across species has ever been observed. In fact, even when human intelligence is applied and scientists have tried to create viable new species, they have hit the walls of genetic limitations. Belief in intelligent design over common descent is not some blind leap of faith, it's the most reasonable explanation for the variety of life we see.

Wait a Second, Isn't This the "God of the Gaps" Fallacy?

Often when I am debating these issues with a non-theist, I will have this line thrown in my direction. It's a standard, go-to phrase for those who think there is no real evidence for design. "God of the gaps" means that when a person of faith comes across something that can't be explained, that person simply invokes a supernatural cause to the "gap" in his or her understanding. This is part of the larger belief which assumes that people of faith aren't critical thinkers and couldn't have possibly come to their position by examining the evidence and making a reasonable decision. The "God of the Gaps" allegation fails here on several levels.

First, "God of the Gaps" is often applied when there is no known evidence for an occurrence and "God" is inserted as the cause. That's not what's happening here. There are good, solid, empirical reasons for believing in design: intelligent code, biological machines, and common design elements all speak to an intelligent designer. It is the evolutionist who has no evidence for the natural forces position: no way to explain the origin of life, a fossil record that doesn't match the theory, no explanation for complex systems or the complex DNA code that brings them about. The only "gap" here is in the naturalist's evidence.

Henry Gee, the chief science writer for *Nature,* writes, "To take a line of fossils and claim they represent a lineage is not a scientific hypothesis that can be tested, but an assertion that carries the same validity as a bedtime story – amusing, perhaps even instructive, but not scientific."[9]

Second, "God of the Gaps" seems to make the assumption that only theists have a bias. I find it so hypocritical when I am debating someone on these issues, and upon finding that I am a theist, they often write me off because I am a person "of faith." What does that matter? My belief system doesn't change the evidence of design in the slightest. Either the evidence supports a belief or it does not. Period. Why assume that theists have a bias while evolutionists are purely objective? This is hardly the case. The real question lies in *why* a person has a bias, not *if* they have one. Is the bias because of the evidence or in spite of it?

The truth is that evolution is far more philosophy than empirical science. It's far more a worldview than a description of the actual origin and variety of life. Often times, when I'm charged with the "God of the Gaps" fallacy, I simply recite the evidence and return the same charge, "Science of the gaps." Many cling to Darwinism in hopes that someday, someone will discover the magic missing link, or natural force, or some other unknown key that will finally give some credibility to their position. But science, real science, is a search for causes, no matter where those causes come from.

The truth is that evolution is far more philosophy than empirical science. It's far more a worldview than a description of the actual origin and variety of life.

There are only two types of causes: natural and intelligent. The evidence we have points strongly to an intelligent cause for life on Earth.

Walter Bradley, who co-authored the ground-breaking work *The Mystery of Life's Origin,* writes, "There doesn't seem to be the potential of finding a [natural explanation] for the origin of life. I think people who believe that life emerged naturalistically need to have a great deal more faith than people who reasonably infer that there's an intelligent designer." [10]

A Call for Civility

I grew up in the great southwest and was surrounded by western culture and legend. Wyatt Earp, William H. Bonney (Billy the Kid), and many other legendary figures influenced my imagination. I loved watching John Wayne movies and TV shows like High Chaparral and Bonanza. As a kid, I had the opportunity to visit some of the places where these western movies and TV shows were filmed. I remember walking onto the set of High Chaparral and being deeply disappointed. Everything was fake. Oh, they made the town look real on television, but up close and personal it was just a facade—literally. Storefronts propped up by scaffolding. Chairs made of balsa wood (so they broke easily in bar fights). Nothing was how it appeared. I walked down the main street of that western "town" being upset at how I was tricked.

I feel the same way about evolution. I feel I was tricked. An over exaggerated fossil record. Falsified embryonic development. Historic "discoveries" that were complete hoaxes and scams. As I got closer to the "evidence," nothing was really as it appeared. I began to see a new world emerging. A new world of order, design, and intelligence that logically pointed to a supernatural origin and explanation. To me, the evidence is clear and undeniable. The amazing universe we live in, the life that surrounds us, has *no* natural explanation. However, not everyone sees the evidence the way I do. I have very good friends who are not theists. They hold a naturalistic worldview. We can have intelligent conversation about our beliefs, remain confident in our differences, and stay friends. Sadly though, such civility is rare. This topic is a very emotional one and often brings about heated debates. I've been involved in many chat rooms and debate threads where the conversation turns ugly. I have been called many names and insulted more times than I can count. "Ignorant," "stupid," "idiot," and much worse not fit for publication. This is not one-sided by any means. I have seen theists do the same. I believe we can, and should, do better. There is no doubt that the debate over origins is an emotional one, but we, as intelligent people, should be able to present our opinions, share our points of view, and examine and present our opinion of the evidence without sinking to personal attacks. If we need to, let's agree to disagree and be civil about it.

Let's review the growing list of attributes the evidence reveals about the creator of the universe.

The Creator is:

Powerful — this is obvious from the size and scope of the universe — which came from nothing.

Spaceless — because it created space, the supernatural cause must exist outside of space.

Timeless — because it created time, the supernatural cause must exist outside of time.

Independent of creation — this is based on logic and reason. The creator cannot be part of creation that came from nothing. The creator must be outside of and independent of that creation.

Personal—to change a state of absolute nothingness into something requires volition, and volition is a choice. Choices are made by intelligent beings, not by random forces.

Intelligent — The remarkable design of the universe requires a super intelligent being to conceive and construct it. We are clearly talking about a being and not an impersonal force.

Purposed — The well-designed universe isn't just here; it appears designed to produce intelligent life. It has purpose and that stems from a purposeful Designer.

Given the evidence from biology we can also add:

Life-Giver — The gap between living and non-living is beyond words. The power, intelligence, purpose, and design to bring about a living being from non-living matter is supernatural.

Chapter Summary

1. Biology is the study of life on Earth and its origins. There are two, and only two, possible causes for life: natural and supernatural.

2. Stanley Miller and others have tried to replicate the theorized beginning of life on Earth, but all have failed to do so. We're supposed to believe that what has yet to be accomplished with intelligence could have happened by accident.

3. Evolution/Darwinism/Naturalism attempts to explain the origin and variety of life through purely natural causes, relying on the mechanisms of mutation and natural selection to do so.

4. The uncooperative fossil record, the undeniable evidence of information as the source of all life, the existence of biological machines, and the principle of common design all provide strong evidence against a natural origin and for intelligent design.

Tough Question 5

How Am I Aware?

CHAPTER 10

Only simpletons believe everything they're told! The wise carefully consider their steps. PROVERBS 14:15

"The brain is just a computer made of meat"
MARVIN MINSKY

2:14 A.M. AUGUST 29TH, 1997. This time stamp may not mean much, but it's a significant key in the movie series, *Terminator*. In the original movie, this is the time and date that Skynet, the computer built to maintain America's defensive systems, becomes self-aware and launches an attack on humans. While the date and time change in successive films, this plot line is critical to the movie's story; an inanimate, non-living computer system gains self-awareness and critical thinking skills — and then, of course, tries to wipe out humanity.

This makes for an exciting movie, and I'm a big fan of the *Terminator* series, but could this actually happen? Is it possible for non-living material to simply come alive and then take an even larger step and develop into "being" status, to become aware? Alive and aware? These are the two things that make us human. They make us different. Could such inexplicable and profound states really come about by accident?

For the atheist, the issue isn't *can* it happen, it *has* to happen! It's the only possible way for the materialistic worldview to explain life. Life had to spontaneously erupt from non-living chemicals. Awareness had to somehow dawn on a creature formerly driven by instinct and stimulus-response mechanisms.

In one of my favorite ***Far Side cartoons,*** *a wife amoeba says to her husband amoeba, "Stimulus response, stimulus response, don't you ever think?!" Not only can we think, we can reason.*

Please use that unbelievable, incredible power of reasoning we all have for just a moment and think about the incredible hurdles the atheist has to leap to simply get to this question.

First, the incredible expanse of time and space, all matter, simply came into existence under its own power out of absolutely nothing. There is an event, but with no cause?

Next, out of all this massive chaos, came incredible complexity, precision, and order so mind boggling we don't even have a number large enough to describe the odds. There is tremendous fine-tuning, but no fine tuner?

Then, amazingly, seemingly miraculously, from the lifeless, inhospitable planet we call Earth, life—poof—simply happened. We weren't there to see it. We can't replicate it. But the atheist is forced to believe that non-living chemicals under random forces could actually *come alive*. There is life, but no life-giver?

Then somehow, some way, life developed to such a point, like Skynet, that it "wakes up" and became a self-thinking, self-aware being, with not just a brain, but now a mind. A thinking being, but not born from a thinking being? A rational being, but not created by a rational being?

These are truly enormous problems for the atheist to explain.

We have explored three very tough questions in previous chapters. We've looked at the massive amounts of evidence regarding the origin of the universe, the incredible fine-tuning in the universe, and biology and life. All of these give strong support for the belief in the existence of a powerful, life-giving creator. In this chapter, we're going to explore how rational awareness is another clue in the chain of evidence that supports this premise.

The Dilemma – 1 Part or more?

In the 1939 classic *The Wizard of Oz*, Ray Bolger, playing the part of the Scarecrow, sings a now familiar lament, "If I Only Had a Brain." When I lock my keys in my truck or leave home without my wallet, I often wonder the same thing. The real question is not whether we have brains. We know we do. We can see them. Study them. Dissect them. Research them. The real question isn't do I have a brain, it's do I have a mind?

To make sure we are all on the same page, let's define those two elements.

The brain is the portion of the vertebrate central nervous system that is enclosed within the cranium. It's the primary center for the regulation and control of bodily activities, receiving and interpreting sensory impulses, and transmitting information to the muscles and body organs. Stated more simply, the brain is an incredibly powerful biological computer that "runs" the rest of the body.

The computing power and speed of the human brain is staggering. Even the most impressive supercomputers can't hold a candle to the three pound wonder inside our skulls. Consider the experiment computer scientists from Japan and Germany undertook in August of 2013. They hooked up 82,000 of the most powerful processors in the world to simulate one second of the brain's computing power. Here are the numbers: The computer scientists recreated 1.73 billion virtual nerve cells and 10.4 trillion synapses, each of which contained 24 bytes of memory. The simulation took 40 minutes of real, "biological" time to produce one virtual second. Billions and trillions of simulated neurons and synapses is nothing to sneeze at, but keep in mind how that equates to only one percent of what's going on in our noggins.[1] Did you catch that? This amazing display of computing power and speed, from the fastest and most powerful computer at the time, took forty minutes to simulate, for one second, just one percent of what the brain is capable of. Our brains are amazing! The atheist believes this kind of computing power came about by accident, while our most intelligent minds haven't yet come close to creating such a computer.

As amazing as the brain is, the mind is much more intriguing.

The mind is the element of personhood that enables us to be aware of the world and our experiences — to think and to feel the faculty of consciousness, feelings, values, convictions, and reasoning.

The brain and the mind are two very different components. The question arises as to the reality and origin of the mind. Is the mind simply a function of the brain? If so, why can we not even begin to explain or understand the link? Or is the functioning of the mind yet another clue to our supernatural design?

As we have seen so far, the evidence supports a supernatural origin to the universe and it supports a supernatural origin to life. Does the evidence also support a supernatural origin of our consciousness? Do we have a soul in addition to our body?

Huge Implications

The implications of this question are enormous. If I'm simply and purely a physical being, then there is no need to look for evidence for supernatural involvement. If my consciousness, my feelings, my ability to engage in introspection, the development of values and convictions, can all be explained by physical processes, then this part of the case is closed. However, if the evidence shows that there is a sharp distinction between my brain and my mind, then we need to look for another explanation.

Let's take a closer look at the implications for each position.

If materialism, or physicalism, is true (that is, we are purely physical and material bodies and nothing more) then that leads to very important conclusions that must also be true.First, if physicalism is true, I really have no conscious awareness and am only tricked by my brain into believing I do. In a purely physical world, where everything has a physical origin and material composition, then you can see, touch, smell, and locate everything. Every star, atom, tree, cell, everything, can be identified and photographed. Even the wind, which is invisible to the naked eye, is made of elements, has atomic weight, and we can identify its cause. But you cannot locate your consciousness. You cannot see or touch your mind. Therefore, it is either a myth or it has another explanation.

Secondly, if physicalism is true, there would be no free will. If I'm a purely physical being run by purely chemical processes, then I have no responsibility for what those may cause me to do. Whether I care for the poor and needy or engage in genocide, those behaviors are out of my control and are simply the result of random physical processes. Atheists are forced by their worldview to adopt this belief. I haven't yet met an atheist that doesn't believe we should be held accountable for our actions. But if my actions are purely the result of physical processes, then how can I be held responsible? If you take the possibility of the supernatural out of the universe, then the entire history of the universe has been physical forces leading to physical reactions. Physical causes leading to physical effects.

Physicalism is a philosophical position holding that everything which exists is no more extensive than its physical properties.

Water is overheated to become steam which condenses and falls to the ground as rain—a physical process. A dead body falls to the ground and is reclaimed by the soil to provide nutrients for the plants which grow to feed the animals—a physical process. And yet, somehow, miraculously, amidst all these purely physical processes, there emerged an unexplained, immaterial reality that we know to be consciousness and a free will. While *your* consciousness and free will may be abstract to me, my own is very real to me, as yours is to you. You are very well aware of your own free will. You can stop reading this page anytime you want. You could go out and ride a bike or rob a store or volunteer at a shelter or...the possibilities are endless and you get to decide. How is it that you decide? Because you have free will and no one could convince you otherwise. So, if you have free will, then you are much more than simply random chemical processes. Your own intuition and experience tell you that you are driven by much more than purely physical processes. You are a mind housed in a body.

The third implication has eternal consequences. If we are purely physical beings, with no mind or consciousness, then there is no existence after physical death. The Bible, along with many other belief systems, declares that we are both physical *and* non-physical beings. Many believe that after our physical death, our mind, will, and emotions — our "soul" — lives on. But if we have no mind, no soul, then eternal life is just another myth.

Those are three implications of the atheist's reality. But implications are not real evidence. Your own self-awareness and free will are strong evidence for the reality of your mind and soul, but is there more evidence from the world of science and medicine? You bet! Let's take a look at some.

Evidences for the Mind

While the evidence for the nature and reality of the mind and soul is not as abundant as the evidence for the "hard" sciences of cosmology, astronomy, and biology, there still exists a growing body that leads to the reasonable conclusion that you are more than just a "computer made of meat."

The Montreal Procedure

Wilder Penfield, the Spokane, WA native and world famous Canadian neurosurgeon, was a groundbreaking force in the treatment of epileptic patients. While they were under no or only local anesthetic, Dr. Penfield would probe the patient's brain to try to locate areas affected by the seizures. What he found along the way was fascinating. As he probed along the brain, he learned he could cause the patient to raise an arm, or clench a fist or blink, among many other physical responses. In doing so, he was able to begin to "map" the brain's physical functions. In his classic work *The Mystery of the Mind,* he recorded many of his findings. What was interesting to Penfield is that the patient would cite the doctor as the cause of the movement: "I didn't do that, you did." [2] The patient saw himself as having an existence separate from his body. Our mind and our body, though connected, are not the same thing. They are separate entities. And here's the real key — no matter how much Penfield probed the cerebral cortex, 'There is no place...where electrical stimulation will cause a patient to believe or decide." [3]

The implications of this are astounding. The world's leading neurosurgeon, who probed the entirety of the human brain in hundreds of patients and mapped the brain for countless physical functions, found no place where values, convictions, beliefs, and moral decisions are made. That's because those higher thoughts are not made in the material brain, they are crafted in the immaterial mind. The brain can cause me to lift my hand, but only in the mind can I embrace generosity. The brain can cause me to move my lips, but only in the mind can I choose to be kind. My brain may control the functions of my body, but in my mind I decide the kind of person I am.

Dream On

Another source of evidence for the separation of the brain and the mind is in our dreams. A physical manifestation of dreams is R.E.M., or Rapid Eye Movement. When a person is dreaming, the eyes dart back and forth under the lids. In dream studies, the brain waves drastically change when a person goes from a non-dreaming to a dreaming state. The different parts of the brain begin firing and the EEG comes alive. The researcher knows the subject is dreaming, but has no idea what the subject is dreaming *about*. To find out, she has to wake the subject and ask. The dream can't be seen, charted, graphed, or recorded. All we know is what the brain is doing, i.e. firing synapses. But we have no idea what the *mind* is doing. Only the dreamer can tell us what the dream was about. In fact, that is key right there. The brain isn't *about* anything. It is simply an electrically charged, organically based, magnificent biological computer system, but it isn't *about* anything. It is our mind that infuses our lives with meaning, purpose, and values.

Clear Interdependence

I have had people challenge me on the mind/brain question with the following: "The mind must be connected to the brain, because the brain influences much of the mind." They then lay out the "facts" for their case, such as brain surgery patients whose personalities are altered after portions of the brain are removed or head trauma victims who change a bit after a portion of their brain is damaged. I don't argue against either of those clear examples. The mind and the brain are clearly connected. However, connection is a far cry from being the same thing. Certainly the brain influences the mind and damage to the brain can alter a person's personality and behavior. The reverse is true as well. The mind influences the brain (and the body for that matter). Countless studies show how thought patterns such as worry, anger, bitterness, and fear physically alter the brain's pathways. In other words, the trains of thought chosen by our conscious minds actually "rewire" the pathways of the physical brain and affect our bodies.

Just focusing our minds on the problems that stress us out can have serious consequences. Stress has been strongly linked to a persistently elevated blood pressure and heart rate, which raises your risk of cardiovascular disease, which is already the leading cause of death in the developed world. Stress reduces the protective fluids in the lining of the digestive system, exacerbating the risk and severity of ulcers and other digestive disorders. A depressed immune system makes it harder for your body to fight off all sorts of diseases, including cancer, or battle them once you do get sick. Chronic stress impairs the formation of new, fast-growing cells, like bone and hair. Worry a lot, for a long time, and you can go bald. Chronic stress reduces your ability to form some new memories, and recall others. At high levels, stress literally dumbs you down. As Dr. Adler says, "If you don't relax, you're going to worry yourself to death." [4]

Take a quick glance at the list above once again. Heart disease, lower immunity, stomach problems, and baldness all can be caused by stress. Focusing the *mind* towards a concentrated thinking, on problems can lead to stress, which can very negatively affect the health of the body. These symptoms aren't the result of a malfunctioning brain; they are the result of a negatively fixated mind. This isn't a brain/body connection, it's a mind/body connection.

Now I'm stressed out about too much stress!

The evidence clearly indicates that the mind and brain are distinct from one another. They are certainly connected and influence one another, but it's quite obvious they are not the same thing.

The Mind and God

A growing body of medical evidence and scientific research points to the reasonable conclusion that the immaterial mind is quite different and distinct from the material brain. In addition to that, most of us know intuitively that our mind and our brain are separate entities. We are well aware that we are aware. Certainly there are those who believe their decisions are so shaped by biology, life experience, or both, that they don't really see themselves as having a free will, but they are in the minority. Few people are convinced that they are *not* reasoning beings with a free will to think as they please.

How did our consciousness originate?

I know of few atheists who would argue that the mind and brain are the same thing and that we really don't have true consciousness. While some materialists believe that consciousness is merely an illusion that has evolved to help us survive, most, I believe, would concede the distinction.

How does an atheist explain the reality of the mind, then? Simple, it's just the result of a high powered, highly evolved brain. Many believe that our brain, much like Skynet from the *Terminator* movies, grew to such a state of complexity and power that it "woke up" from material unconsciousness to immaterial awareness.

This is the "go to" belief system of the atheist—something from nothing.

> **The universe**—absolutely everything sprang from absolutely nothing.
>
> **Fine tuning** — amazing precision came from utter chaos.
>
> **Life**—poof! Out of nowhere.
>
> **Conscious awareness**—Awake, oh computer made of meat, and know that you just are.

These make for wonderful fairy tales, but aren't much more substantial than that. This is what caused the man called the greatest living American philosopher, Alvin Plantinga, of Notre

Dame to comment, "Things don't look good for Darwinian naturalists." [5]

The truth is that the atheist worldview is simply inadequate to explain anything concerning origins.

It's far more logical and reasonable to believe that where there is an origin, there is an originator.

> **The universe**—it had a beginning, therefore it must have a cause behind it.
>
> **Fine tuning**—when you see great design, look for a great designer.
>
> **Life**—living things give rise to living things.
>
> **Conscious awareness**—look for a super intelligent mind.

The Christian worldview is far more equipped to reasonably explain these phenomena. The God of the Christian story is an intelligent, conscious being, fully capable of choice, thought, values, desires, decisions, feelings, awareness, and purpose. He is also invisible, just like your consciousness is invisible. As we learned in Tough Question #2, God is not limited to the physical world. He lives in it yet outside of it as well. This is how consciousness works. It's no surprise that since we are made "in His image," we take on those same characteristics. I can see your body, but I

> *You are a mind housed in a physical body, not just a body with a brain.*

cannot see the real you. The real you is actually invisible—an immaterial being clothed in the body you see. Nowhere in my body can you find me.

You could take me apart piece by piece and yet my consciousness remains whole. My consciousness activates and animates my body, yet is clearly not limited to it. To put it succinctly, you are a soul housed in a body. You *are* a soul. You *have* a body. It's not difficult to imagine that intelligent, aware, conscious beings would follow in the design of a supremely intelligent, aware, conscious being. Philosopher Stuart Hackett said it better than I ever could: "Selfhood is not explicable in material or physical terms. The essential, spiritual selfhood of man has its only adequate ground in the transcendent spiritual selfhood of God as Absolute Mind. With modest apologies to Descartes: *Cogito, ergo Deus est!* I think, therefore God is!" [6]

Let's review the growing list of attributes that the evidence reveals about the Intelligent Designer.

The Creator is:

> **Powerful** — this is obvious from the size and scope of the universe — which came from nothing.
>
> **Spaceless** — because it created space, the supernatural cause must exist outside of space.
>
> **Timeless** — because it created time, the supernatural cause must exist outside of time.

Independent of creation — this is based on logic and reason. The creator cannot be part of creation that came from nothing. The creator must be outside of and independent of that creation.

Personal—to change a state of absolute nothingness into something requires volition, and volition is a choice. Choices are made by intelligent beings, not by random forces.

Intelligent — The remarkable design of the universe requires a super intelligent being to conceive and construct it. We are clearly talking about a being and not an impersonal force.

Purposed — The well-designed universe isn't just here; it appears designed to produce intelligent life. It has purpose, and that stems from a purposeful Designer.

Life-Giver — The gap between living and non-living is beyond words. The power, intelligence, purpose, and design to bring about a living being from non-living matter is supernatural.

Given the evidence from awareness, we can also add:

Immaterial Mind — Our own conscious awareness, apart from our physical body, is a solid clue that the creator is a consciously aware immaterial being.

Chapter Summary

1. If the entire universe is merely a physical result controlled by physical processes, then we too are merely a physical body controlled by physical processes.

2. However, our own experiences of self-awareness, as well as studies on the mind, show we are more than just our body.

3. Our brain and mind, though linked, are not the same thing. This is proven by studies on epilepsy patients, as well as our own reasoning.

4. My physical brain can account for the functioning of my body, but can't account for compassion, kindness, morality, and love. Those are generated by the mind.

5. You are a mind, a soul, housed in a physical body.

Tough Question 6

Why Do We Care?

Chapter 11

Then a despised Samaritan came along, and when he saw the man, he felt compassion for him. Going over to him, the Samaritan soothed his wounds with olive oil and wine and bandaged them. Then he put the man on his own donkey and took him to an inn, where he took care of him. The Good Samaritan parable Luke 10:25-37

"I do not see why man should not be just as cruel as nature."
Adolf Hitler

I can still hear the smack of his fist hitting her face and I can still see her head thud against the stucco wall. It's a scene I will never forget as long as I live. Thirty years later, it's still as sickening as the day I witnessed it. I was a high school sophomore living in Ruidoso, New Mexico. Ruidoso is a small tourist town nestled high in the southern reaches of the Great Rocky Mountains. Quarter Horse racing in the summer and white powder skiing in the winter bring people from all over the Southwest to this wonderful village. For a kid who loved the outdoors, it was a fantastic place to grow up. It happened on a gorgeous summer afternoon, with filtered sunlight making its way through the Ponderosa Pine and the Quaking Aspen. I passed Jackalope Square on my left. This small shopping area is so named because of the eight foot antlered Jackalope in the center of the parking area. A Jackalope is a mythical creature in the southwest and is a cross between a Jackrabbit and an

Antelope. The Scotts have "Nessie," the northwest has Bigfoot… we have our Jackalope. Ruidoso was a great place to grow up. However, on this particular summer afternoon, I saw a much darker side of life and humanity.

As I made my way past the giant Jackalope, I noticed a conflict brewing across the street at a tavern. A man and a woman just outside the bar door leaned against the wall. He was yelling and she was crying. As he loudly berated her, she slumped down onto her backside and sat next to him and began to weep. I couldn't hear exactly what he was saying, but his tone was angry. What happened next both disgusted and angered me. He turned toward her and began violently punching her in the face. Two very strong emotions welled up in me. First, hatred for the man who would beat on a helpless woman. Second, a strong desire to run across the street and rescue her.

Now, I look back on that scene with much greater clarity. After twenty years of being a counselor, I understand the dynamics of alcohol abuse, relational conflict, and anger issues. But I still must ask the question—why did I care? I didn't know the couple. The woman wasn't a family member or friend or even a friend of a friend. What caused such strong feelings of righteous indignation and a rescue impulse?

This compassion and protective impulse is hardly mine alone. We see examples all around us. Why do strangers rush into burning homes to rescue those trapped inside? Why do we send countless millions of dollars to aid natural disaster victims we've never met? Have we simply been trained to show compassion for those in need or danger, or could those emotions and responses also be clues to something else?

In the rest of this chapter, we'll consider the role compassion plays and see if it adds to the mounting evidence that there is a supernatural cause to all we see. Let's briefly review what we've covered so far.

Using scientific evidence, reason, philosophy, and logic we can reasonably come to the following conclusions:

- Created things come from a creator
- Design comes from a designer
- Life comes from a living being
- Consciousness stems from intelligent consciousness

In this chapter, we will discuss whether our moral code is written by a moral law giver.

Does Morality Exist?

Just last week, I engaged in a healthy debate with an atheist on the topic of faith. She made the statement that people of faith don't have the corner on doing good and that she has lots of atheist friends who are kind and charitable and gracious and that she herself is a good person. I know many non-theists that are quite virtuous. On the other hand, I know many people of faith that have the warmth of a rattlesnake. I conceded her point, but followed up by asking her, "How do you know what "good" is? I mean, how do you measure good and bad unless you have some sort of standard to measure it by? And then, where do you get that standard?"

If there is no God, then there is no real standard of right and wrong. If the entire universe is one giant, amazing stroke of luck, then life itself is an amazing chemical accident, and consciousness is a fascinating by-product of brain power, all of which leaves very little room for the idea of right and wrong. If Darwinism is true, then survival of the fittest should be the rule. While we see many examples of this process at work in nature, it's clear that we are different. In the human experience, we also see touching stories of sacrifice, honor, courage, nobility, and generosity. Above these individual acts of compassion, love, and service is an undeniable reality. Every society everywhere has standards of morality by which they are governed. We call them laws. Why is that the case? Why isn't society just a chaotic free-for-all?

An obvious possible answer to these questions is that there is a moral code written into the human race. If there is a moral law written into humanity, then there must be a moral law giver.

Is there evidence for such a moral code? When I use the word "evidence," I am not referring to scientific evidence. As we learned in previous chapters, not all evidence is "scientific" in nature. The evidence we seek here is of a moral nature. It can't be weighed or tested, and yet it is clearly seen. To suggest that a moral standard exists is to suggest that all people everywhere throughout time have been imbued with a fundamental sense of right and wrong. I won't suggest for a second that we consistently honor that sense of right and wrong, but it does, in fact, exist. Nor will I suggest that the moral code is identical for each culture. That is not the point. The point is that every culture, tribe, society, clan knows that certain things are right and certain things are wrong. The founders of

Point to Ponder

Is there a moral code written into our soul as there is a genetic code written into our bodies?

our nation knew this when Thomas Jefferson wrote about truths that are "self-evident." The lady I was debating showed that she knew it when she talked about being "good." Everyone reading these words knows that generosity is superior to thievery and honesty is more desirable than lying. We know to honor courage and revile cowardice. The man who murders a neighbor is seen very differently from the man who runs into a burning building to save a stranger.

Why? How is it that we all "know" these things?

C.S. Lewis states this observation so eloquently in his classic work, *Mere Christianity*. "Think of a country where people were admired for running away in battle, or where a man felt proud of double-crossing all the people who had been kindest to him. You might just as well try to imagine a country where two and two make five." [1]

This doesn't mean that there aren't difficult moral issues that we wrestle with. This doesn't mean that many people don't ignore or even deny the existence of a standard of right and wrong. It simply means that there are basic principles of right and wrong that we all know to be real, and these are evident in the ways we act and, more importantly, react.

Moral Law is Irrefutable

The relativist, of course, disagrees with this premise. Not wanting to believe that there must be a giver to our moral laws, they assert, "There is no absolute moral law because there is no absolute truth." To which I respond, "Is that absolutely true?" Their statement that there is no absolute truth is, in fact, a statement of absolute truth. If there are no absolute truths, then their statement *must* be absolutely false.

Relativism: the doctrine that knowledge, truth, and morality exist in relation to culture, society, or historical context, and are not absolute.

The thinking person can see the undeniable fact of moral law.

We observe the universality of moral law in how we react when we feel we've been violated. Even the person who stubbornly states that there are no absolute laws and rights enjoys the laws and rights that give them the freedom to take such a stance.

Smash in the window of a relativist's car, steal her stereo, and watch how quickly she values personal property.

Walk into the home of a relativist —as an uninvited stranger — and sit down beside him as he watches a late night sitcom. You will discover how strongly he embraces the value of privacy.

Clean out the bank account of an atheist and give it to his in-laws and watch how fast he pursues the values of justice and fairness.

The evidence is clear. While some may argue against moral truth and law *hypothetically,* they would never deny it when it affects them *personally.* Relativists are like bad poker players; you can tell what they *really* believe when they're dealt a bad hand. It is in these moments that their true beliefs surface.

Relativists are like bad poker players; you can tell what they really believe when they're dealt a bad hand.

Our actions and reactions are strong evidence that moral law is written into the fabric of our moral DNA.

In their fantastic book, *I Don't Have Enough Faith to be an Atheist,* the authors relate a story that highlights my point.

A professor at a major university in Indiana gave his ethics class a term paper assignment. He told the students to write on any ethical topic of their choice and required each student only to properly back up his or her thesis with reasons and documentation.

One student, an atheist, wrote eloquently on the topic of moral relativism. He argued, "All morals are relative. There is no absolute standard of justice or rightness; it's all a matter of opinion. You like chocolate, I like vanilla." And so on. His paper provided both his reasons and his documentation. It was the right length, on time, and stylishly presented in a handsome blue folder.

After the professor read the entire paper, he wrote on the front cover, "F, I don't like blue folders!" When the student got the paper back, he was enraged. He stormed into the professor's office and protested, "F! I don't like blue folders!" That's not fair! That's not right" That's not just! You didn't grade the paper on its merits!"

Raising his hand to quiet the bombastic student, the professor calmly retorted, "Wait a minute. Hold on. I read a lot of papers. Let me see...wasn't your paper the one that said there is no such thing as fairness, rightness, and justice?"

"Yes," the student answered.

> "Then what's this you say about me not being fair, right, and just?" the professor asked. "Didn't your paper argue that it's all a matter of taste? You like chocolate, I like vanilla?"
>
> The student replied, "Yes, that's my view."
>
> "Fine then," the professor responded, "I don't like blue. You get an F!"
>
> Suddenly the light bulb went on in the student's head. He realized that he really did believe in moral absolutes. He at least believed in fairness, rightness, and justice. [2]

More proof of Moral Law

While relativists argue *intellectually* against the idea of an absolute moral law, our *reactions* prove that we believe there is such a thing. Many of the great struggles in our nation's history are the reaction to violations of moral law.

Our Civil War was a response to the violation of human dignity and intrinsic worth. We know that no human being should be treated like property. This is moral law.

The civil rights movement a century later was a continuation of this understanding. Discriminatory laws and practices needed to be changed because treating two groups of people according to two sets of rules is inherently unfair. This is moral law.

We get incensed when we hear of a CEO raiding the trust funds of the frontline workers that built the company. They lose their retirement while he sits on a beach in Italy. We want justice. That is moral law.

I could go on with many more examples. Our entire justice system is built on an understanding of right and wrong. Without moral law, there are no grounds for applauding virtue or punishing vice.

Moral law goes far beyond our nation's laws, however. It extends even to the basic ways we treat each other. Imagine that you're in a long and slowly moving line at the bank. There is only one teller, but you're patiently waiting your turn. All of a sudden, a man enters and passes you and everyone else in line and walks up to the teller. "I'm in a hurry and can't wait. I want to make a deposit." You and I both know what we would most likely be feeling at that moment (and possibly even saying). "Hey buddy, you can go to the back of the line and wait like the rest of us!" The minute he walked past you and demanded his selfish way, a red flag went up and a warning light went off in your head. We know that such behavior is simply not "right." But if there is no God, then there is no right. Not in big matters, like genocide or slavery, or in small matters, like bank line etiquette.

How do you respond to the line cutting violation? Do you internalize the frustration, comment to those in line around you, or speak up to the violator?

However, we know that some things are just "right" and this proves beyond reasonable doubt that there is a standard for things that are "right"—a Law Giver.

Objections to Moral Law

Not so fast, the relativist might say. Just because there is an obvious moral law and countless examples of sacrifice, courage, and compassion to honor, it doesn't necessarily mean it has a supernatural origin.

Why couldn't our illusion of morality have come about just like our illusion of awareness? The usual origin for morality suggested by atheists is the same origin they use for consciousness and life itself—evolution.

The argument goes something like this. Just as time and chance caused life to spring from non-living chemicals, just as time and chance gave rise to the amazing variety of life we see, just as time and chance caused consciousness to "awaken" from mere impulse, given enough time and chance, we developed this reflex we call "morality" to help us get along with one another. It's the survival mechanism we developed to help us live in peace as we propagate our lineage.

The argument continues that though evolution is the survival of the fittest, it also works to provide tribes and clans with the necessary tools to carry on their genes. So morality and the laws that come with it are nothing more than an evolutionary by-product that help us to get along so we can continue to further our species. Some people call this "social evolution" or "social Darwinism."

> *"As evolutionists, we see that no [ethical] justification of the traditional kind is possible. Morality, or more strictly our belief in morality, is merely an adaptation put in place to further our reproductive ends. Hence the basis of ethics does not lie in God's will.... In an*

> *important sense, ethics as we understand it is an illusion fobbed off on us by our genes to get us to cooperate. It is without external grounding."* [3]

You can clearly see the evolutionist's case here. Morality does not have an outside source, "external grounding," but was developed along the evolutionary pathway to further our species. In their opinion, ethics is genetically based.

We have completely mapped the human chromosome. We know how to determine eye color, skin pigmentation, and look for possible generational defects that might be passed on. But we have found *no* genetic character traits. I'm still waiting for them to find the gene for generosity. Where exactly on the genetic map is the marker for courage? Kindness?

Here, the atheist begins to wade into very muddy waters. Those who so passionately cling to "scientific evidence" still wander around blindly in the dark when there is obviously no such evidence to support this claim.

There are several problems with this line of reasoning.

The Personalization of Evolution

I am fascinated by the consistent need for atheists to speak of the evolutionary process in personalized terms. Using terms like "chose" or "selected" or "passed on," they often make evolution sound like...well, a person. Look at the quote above again and note the phrase, "put in place." "Put in place" shows intent, choice, and intelligence. Remember, evolution is not a force, a power, an anything. It is simply the randomness of chance combined with vast expanses of time. It's the variation of genetics being expressed in a gene pool with the less effective ones being weeded out over time due to non-survivability. While we can find the genes for our humanness, our eye color, our hair color, our intelligence, we have no genes for morality.

The idea that evolution "selected" morality or "put in place" a system of ethics to be passed on genetically from one generation to the next doesn't at all fit the concept of natural selection. Chemicals can't think. Protein compounds can't strategize an outcome. They can't have a purpose, or a goal, or a plan. When atheists personalize evolution, they're simply giving it godlike qualities of purpose and design when clearly, it can't have any. This is true whether you are talking about the design of wings for flight or ethics for survivability. Evolution has no power to decide anything.

When atheists personalize evolution, they're simply giving it godlike qualities of purpose and design when clearly, it can't have any.

Mother Teresa vs. Adolf Hitler

Let's pretend for a second that evolution could "select," "put in place," and "pass on" the compassion/morality gene. The gene was "given" to us by evolution so we could better govern ourselves and pass on our genes to the next generation. But doesn't evolution dictate that only the genes of the strongest and best traits are "selected" and the weaker ones "deselected?" Why then do we have countless programs and hospitals for the physically and mentally challenged? Why do we care for the dying and elderly? Why do the handicapped get parking spots near the front of the store?

If evolution were true, none of these things should exist. If social evolution were true, then our evolved sense of law and morality would only apply to making sure the "fittest" survived. In addition to that, there's no reason for us to really care for those we have never met and who have no impact on our lives. If evolution is true, there is no reason to send rice to the starving in Ethiopia or give money to drill wells for children dying of thirst in Kenya. In a world of limited resources, evolution and humanism dictate that we look after only those who can help us succeed: our family, our race, our line, our clan and at most, our country. We shouldn't care about others. But, the obvious fact is, we do care — a lot! We greatly value compassion and denounce those who lack it.

Adolf Hitler is one of the most reviled men in history. His adamant stance that the Aryan race was superior and that inferior races should be exterminated led to the genocide of over 6 million Jews, along with the deaths of millions of others. He is a blight in the annals of history. Where did Hitler get such a view? Well, from evolution of course. His actions are the logical outcome of a worldview that excludes God and where natural selection rules the day.

Here are his own words:

> "If Nature does not wish that weaker individuals should mate with the stronger, she wishes even less that a superior race should intermingle with an inferior one; because in such a case all her efforts, throughout hundreds of thousands of years, to establish an evolutionary higher stage of being, may thus be rendered futile.

> But such a preservation goes hand-in-hand with the inexorable law that it is the strongest and the best who must triumph and that they have the right to endure. He who would live must fight. He who does not wish to fight in this world, where permanent struggle is the law of life, has not the right to exist." [4]

Hitler's social genocide was based on the principles he found in Darwin's evolutionary theory of survival of the fittest. The link is undeniable.

Now read what Charles Darwin said in his history-making work:

> "At some future period, not very distant as measured by centuries, the civilised races of man will almost certainly exterminate, and replace, the savage races throughout the world....The break between man and his nearest allies will then be wider, for it will intervene between man in a more civilised state, as we may hope, even than the Caucasian, and some ape as low as a baboon, instead of as now between the negro or Australian and the gorilla." [5]
>
> [Just so there is no doubt, Darwin is claiming that whites will exterminate blacks.]

Sir Arthur Keith was a British anthropologist, an atheistic evolutionist and an anti-Nazi, but he drew this chilling conclusion:

> "The German Führer, as I have consistently maintained, is an evolutionist; he has consciously sought to make the practice of Germany conform to the theory of evolution."[6]

I'm not suggesting that believing in evolution leads to embracing genocide. Hitler also did refer to God wanting to kill Jews (although that was certainly done to appease the religious in his nation and not because of his personal belief system). To be sure, there were many streams of thought that played into Nazi racism and the holocaust, but to say that Darwinism played no role, or even an insignificant role, is absurd.

On the other hand, the religious and non-religious alike praise Mother Teresa. Born Agnes Gonxha Bojaxhiu in 1910, she spent the vast majority of her adult life serving the "untouchable" class of Calcutta, India. She gave herself almost completely to the poorest of the poor. The lepers, the orphans, the poor, those whom society simply ignored or abused. She worked tirelessly to make sure they had a meal and a home. During her lifetime, Mother Teresa was named eighteen times in the annual Gallup Most Admired Man and Woman poll as one of the ten women around the world who Americans respected most. In 1999, a poll of Americans ranked her first in Gallup's List of Most Widely Admired People of the Twentieth Century. She won the Nobel Peace Prize in 1979 and asked that the money be given to the poor in India. She was truly a remarkable woman.

Many people give themselves sacrificially for what they believe, and that in itself doesn't make their belief system true. Both Hitler and Mother Teresa had very passionate beliefs that drove their worldviews and lifestyles. Why do we praise her and revile him? This is a clue to our morality, our compassion, and our intrinsic worth. We *know* that her life is a better one! But how is it that we "know" such a thing?

The problem relativists run into is that most of them revile such behavior as Hitler's and praise Mother Teresa-like qualities without a moral basis to do so. They know some things are "wrong" and others are "right." But if there truly is no absolute right and wrong, and we just make it up as we go along, then why should some actions be condemned while others extolled? Yes, the atheists truly painted themselves into a corner with this one.

This doesn't mean that atheists and relativists can't be moral or kind or "good." As I stated earlier, I know many who are. They simply have no basis for being so, and by the same token, have no standard for condemning those who are not.

Absolute Law is Discovered, Not Defined

It happened again! I was just watching some pre-coverage of President Obama's second inauguration, and the journalist was interviewing an atheist on the use of the Bible in the ceremony. The atheist represented the point that the Bible shouldn't be used in such a ceremony. He went on to say that our nation didn't get our moral principles from the Bible (which is, of course, absurd and this man has no concept of our history, but that's for another discussion) and then he made the following statement: "Religion gets our morality from us. We don't get our morality from religion. We create morality." Of course, my ears perked up when he said this because I was in the middle of writing this chapter.

Let's assume for a moment that statement is true. Let's assume that all the moral laws in all the world's religions were fused into those religions by the very men who created them. Even if that were the case, it still doesn't address the fact that we were internally governed by those moral codes long before they were ever written down. We didn't "create morality" as this man was trying to assert; we discovered it. We discover it when it's violated and our internal response screams, "That's wrong!"

When a child is abused or the weak are trampled or our own property is stolen, we "know" that something has been violated. When we see great acts of sacrifice, nobility or heroism we "know" that behavior is to be championed. It's in these countless human interactions and the heat and friction and conflict that come from them that we discover the undeniable moral codes written deep in our souls.

Absolute Morals vs. Changing Behavior

Another common argument of the relativist is to point out the changing of morals and behavior from one generation to the next. If morals were absolute, they argue, then morality wouldn't change over time. In our country, slavery was once accepted by our government, many of our citizens, and even many churches, but now it's soundly and rightfully condemned. Some use examples like this to argue that morality changes over time and therefore is not absolute. Of course, this line of reasoning makes no logical sense. I would never suggest that we, as a race, are good at honoring the absolute laws that are evident in every culture through every time period in history. We often reject right and wrong to do what benefits us in the moment. The bank robber knows that stealing other people's money is wrong, but greed has driven him to steal anyway.

It's ludicrous for the atheist to attempt to use changing behavior and cultural trends as evidence against moral law. Some even go so far as to say that we change morality choices because it's in our best interest to do so. Of course, we don't always do what's in our best interest. Our nation's obesity problem is proof enough that we often select behaviors we know are bad for us simply because it's easier.

Just because one person, or generation, or even a group of people violates certain principles and embraces others, does not change the obvious fact that they exist. The mere existence of right and wrong, not whether we accept or deny it, is all the proof necessary.

The Relativist's Two-Story Universe

Shaeffer's analogy of the modern man's two-story universe is a good word picture of the dilemma of the atheist, as well as the confident position of the theist.

In the drab basement of the "home" is the material world, with no acceptance of the possibility of the supernatural. Here everything is finite, natural, and doomed. Here, life has no meaning, no purpose, and no value. Life is absurd, but the atheist has no choice, due to his worldview, but to live here. Like a basement, it's dark, dank, smelly, and ugly. Of course, the atheist can't happily live in such a dreary place. As often as possible, and hoping that nobody is paying attention, he sneaks up the stairs into the beautiful upper story, where the theist lives. Here, he's surrounded by the grandeur and majesty of the Creator. These rooms are brightened by beauty, meaning, compassion, generosity, kindness, value, and purpose. Even though he has no right, the atheist attempts to steal these virtues and smuggle them back downstairs to light up his living space.

The point is this: If there is no God, then there are no values, morals, and meaning. But we can't live consistently and happily believing that life is meaningless. So the atheist is forced to pretend that life has value and meaning. This is entirely inconsistent with his worldview, for without God, man and the universe have no significance.

The atheist can't stand to live in the ugly basement of his purposeless, meaningless worldview, so he sneaks upstairs to borrow purpose, value, meaning, and significance from the light-filled rooms of the theist.

The theist, however, has no such dilemma. Recognizing the vast evidence and clues pointing to the existence of an uncaused, timeless, intelligent, moral being, the theist comfortably takes his place in the upper story and enjoys its beauty, majesty, mystery, and order.

Let's review the growing list of attributes that the evidence reveals about the Intelligent Designer.

The Creator is:

> **Powerful** — this is obvious from the size and scope of the universe — which came from nothing.
>
> **Spaceless** — because it created space, the supernatural cause must exist outside of space.
>
> **Timeless** — because it created time, the supernatural cause must exist outside of time.
>
> **Independent of creation** — this is based on logic and reason. The creator cannot be part of creation that came from nothing. The creator must be outside of and independent of that creation.
>
> **Personal**—to change a state of absolute nothingness into something requires volition, and volition is a choice. Choices are made by intelligent beings, not by random forces.
>
> **Intelligent** — The remarkable design of the universe requires a super intelligent being to conceive and construct it. We are clearly talking about a being and not an impersonal force.

Purposed — The well-designed universe isn't just here; it appears designed to produce intelligent life. It has purpose and that stems from a purposeful Designer.

Life-Giver — The gap between living and non-living is beyond words. The power, intelligence, purpose, and design to bring about a living being from non-living matter is supernatural.

Immaterial Mind — Our own conscious awareness apart from our physical body is a solid clue that the creator is a consciously aware immaterial being.

Given the evidence from awareness we can also add:

Moral Law Giver — The overwhelming evidence of the existence of right and wrong, good and evil, is another clue to the character of God. God is a moral being and has woven a moral code into the very fabric of our being.

Chapter Summary

1. Moral laws and standards are seen in every culture throughout history.

2. Those that would claim that there is no such thing as morality betray their beliefs when their own sense of right and wrong is threatened or violated.

3. Evolution can't answer why moral expressions like generosity, kindness, forgiveness, and sacrifice exist. We care for many we've never met and can't do anything for us.

4. How we feel about Hitler and Mother Teresa give a stark historical example that we "know" some things are right and some things are wrong.

5. The atheist can't stand to live in the ugly basement of his purposeless, meaningless worldview, so he sneaks upstairs to borrow purpose, value, meaning, and significance from the light-filled rooms of the theist.

Tough Question 7

Why is There So Much Pain?

Chapter 12

Weeping may last through the night, but joy comes with the morning. Psalm 30:5

"The Christian worldview is an impractical, even phony, view of the Cosmos because it embraces a God who is either incapable of stopping evil and suffering, and he is therefore not omnipotent, or is unwilling to do so and therefore a devil!"

Email from a Skeptic

Why So Much Pain?

As I shared earlier, I spent my high school years amongst the towering pines of the small tourist town of Ruidoso, New Mexico. However, my early childhood years were in the desert town of Alamogordo, New Mexico. Alamogordo, or "Alamo" as we all called it. It is in the high desert and very close to Holloman Air Force Base and White Sands Missile Range. White Sands is most famous for being the home of Trinity Site, where the first atomic weapon was detonated. My father was a veteran of the Army Air Corps (the predecessor to our modern day Air Force). At the time of my birth, he worked as a Civil Servant on many military and government projects in the area. We had a nice house on Pecan Avenue and my parents were building a nice life together. Then, when I was eighteen months old, my dad had his first stroke. This unforeseen, unpredictable event shattered our lives and turned our world upside down.

My dad went from being the very intelligent bread winner, provider, father, husband, and leader of our home to the one who needed the most care and attention. This took a huge toll on my mom and left an enormous vacuum in my life. He continued to live with us and my mom cared for him. I was so young that I didn't know he was my dad. He was just the guy who wandered around the house and yard. The stroke robbed him of the ability to retrieve short-term memory. He could tell me about his childhood and even his time in the military, but he didn't know who I was or where his bedroom was located. He taught me how to ride a bike, swing on a swing and throw a baseball, but had no idea I was his son. I have some very fond memories of the man who was my dad while neither of us knew it.

One nice summer evening, I went out into the backyard to play with him and found him lying face down on the ground. He'd had his second stroke. My mother cried by his bedside and pricked his legs with needles to see if and where he had feeling. He died later that evening. I still remember the ambulance taking him away as I stood in our front yard crying. I was nine.

Like many of you reading this, I've lost several loved ones. My first significant experience with death was that of the man I would afterward learn was my father. In the ensuing years, I experienced much more pain and loss. Numerous aunts, uncles, and close family friends passed away in my junior high and high school years. My next younger brother, Carl, was killed in a motorcycle accident the week before his high school graduation. He was our school's valedictorian and was supposed to be the best man at my wedding in three months. I got the news from my mom, hung up the phone, and wept uncontrollably. I have never cried so hard in all my life. How could God allow such a thing to happen to such a fine young man? I was furious with God.

The number one question of resistance I receive concerning the nature and existence of God is about the reality of suffering and evil. While many reject God because of the misinformation from science, for many others, the mere existence of so much hurt and pain is all the evidence they need to deny the existence of a sovereign God.

If I were ordering these nine questions due to the amount of questions I receive, this one would have been at the front of the book. While the first six are intellectual and philosophical in nature, this one is very emotional. I was tempted to begin my book with this question, but felt it necessary to address the evidence in a logical order. I thought it necessary to prove that God exists before I can address being angry with Him.

As we look at compassion, I'll do my best to address this very difficult and legitimate question.

I'd like to take you back to Trinity Site. As I mentioned above, I grew up very near this historic place and learned early its importance in human history. Before that first atomic detonation on July 16, 1945, the super-secret "Manhattan Project" at Los Alamos labs in Northern New Mexico was tasked with learning how to split the atom and harness its power. Since that problem was solved, atomic power has been used in two very different directions. Later in 1945, the United States dropped two atomic bombs on the Japanese cities of Hiroshima and Nagasaki. An unbelievable level of death, pain, and destruction was unleashed. The age of atomic power was upon us. In the decades that followed, we amassed enough atomic weaponry to destroy all life on Earth several times over. However, nuclear power is not inherently evil. It has very positive benefits as well.

There are 104 nuclear facilities in thirty-one states in the United States, and they provide roughly 20% of all U.S. electricity. Nuclear energy is by far the most efficient of all energy-producing sources and is far cleaner than oil, gas, or coal, as it releases *no* emissions into our atmosphere. In fact, nuclear energy produces 63% of all U.S. emission-free electricity. As far as cost, nuclear energy is 50% cheaper than coal and half as expensive as natural gas. In addition to the electrical-generating power of nuclear energy, many of the submarines and ships that keep our waters safe are powered by this source.

Is nuclear power evil and destructive or is it helpful and beneficial? The answer, of course, is it depends on how it is used.

At this point you may be asking, "How does nuclear energy have anything to do with pain and suffering and the existence of God?" Please stay with me here.

All the evidence we've looked at so far points to the very reasonable likelihood that there is a timeless, uncaused, personal, rational, intelligent being who, it appears, has designed us in His image. This means we, too, are rational, personal, intelligent beings who have been granted by our Creator an unbelievable power. This gift is the power of choice. Like nuclear energy, this power is inherently neither good nor evil, it just is. The manner in which this awesome power is used determines whether the outcomes are beneficial or devastating.

The greatest gift we have been given is the power of choice. Every moment of every day we get to decide how to live, speak, act, and react.

The Power of Choice

I can't imagine the pain! The loss of a child is a parent's worst nightmare. As a father of two, the idea of either of my children being ripped from me in a violent manner is unthinkable. On December 14, 2012, that nightmare became reality for twenty families in Newtown, Connecticut. 9:35 a.m. that morning, 20-year-old Adam Peter Lanza shot his way through the locked security doors and into the school. Adam had already shot and killed his mother, Nancy, earlier that morning and he was determined to continue his rampage. As shots rang out, teachers screamed and children ran. Ten minutes and one-hundred shots later, it was over. Adam had killed twenty beautiful children and six adults who tried to save them. Adam took his own life as first responders began to arrive. The horror was over, but the grief, pain, and questions were just beginning.

What caused Adam to do such an unspeakable thing? We'll never really know what caused him to snap that day. Those reasons died with him. But I do know this—Adam made a choice that day. He exercised the greatest power God has given us, the power to choose. He took whatever anger, frustration, and perceived offenses he had and decided to form them into murderous rage. It all boils down to his choice. Adam, however, was not the only one to make dramatic choices that day.

Anne Marie Murphy, a teacher's aide who worked with special-needs students, shielded six-year-old Dylan Hockley with her body, trying to protect him from the bullets that killed them both. Paraprofessional Rachel D'Avino, who had been employed at the school and was working with a special-needs student for a little more than one week, also died trying to protect her students. Choice. When faced with running and possible safety or trying to protect the children entrusted to their care, they chose the latter: Courageous, heroic, inspiring choices.

Each sunrise, God Himself hands us two gifts, the gift of that day and the gift of choice. My actions and reactions are my choice. My words are my choice. I choose the thoughts I dwell on and the attitude I embrace. The power of choice is the most powerful force in the world. Like atomic energy, it can be used for tremendous destruction or for incredible good. Today, you and I get to determine how we each handle this power.

As a counselor, I've had the sacred agony of helping many families walk through the grief and pain of losing a loved one. I understand the "How could a good God allow such a thing?" question that often comes out of such loss. In twenty years of counseling, I have dealt with just about every type of personal loss, tragedy and violence that one can imagine. I have tremendous compassion for people in that situation because I've walked through that same valley many times. I fully understand that most of the time, this question isn't a purely intellectual one. It is deeply personal and deeply emotional. While we certainly don't like the reality of the pain of life when it touches us and those we love, it's very often, not always, the logical consequence of the choices we or others make. I will address other sources of pain and loss, like disease and natural disasters in a moment, but first we need to address the primary source of them — our choices.

There is no rational conflict between the existence of a supremely good creator and the existence of pain and death. Those two things are not mutually exclusive. The former exists because He is timeless and uncaused and the latter exists because He granted us the moral freedom of choice.

The Great Risk

The biblical story of Adam and Eve in the garden illuminates this truth. Whether you believe this story to be literal or allegorical, the principle is the same. Mankind was created and given an absolutely perfect environment in which to live. They enjoyed a perfect relationship with each other. They had a perfect relationship with the Creator. Everything was perfect and they had the incredible power of choice. Then they chose poorly, and that poor choice wreaked havoc on all their relationships. Those poor choices, and all of mankind's subsequent poor choices, are the source of most of the pain, loss, and tragedy that we endure.

While the "Why is there so much pain?" question is a natural one, it's fairly easy to answer. The next deeper question is, "Why would the Creator give us such a power if He knew it would cause so much hurt?" In other words, why would God take such a risk? I believe the answer lies in the flip side to the "pain" question.

While the power of choice can, and is often, used for great harm, it is also, undeniably, the source of incredible acts of generosity, compassion, nobility, courage, and above all, love. While we wrestle with the pain questions, we often lose sight of the tremendous good that's done by billions of people around the world.

There is no rational conflict between the existence of a supremely good creator and the existence of pain and death. Those two things are not mutually exclusive. The former exists because He is timeless and uncaused, and the latter exists because He granted us the moral freedom of choice.

I witness this beautiful side of humanity every day of my life and am still moved by it.

Roger (not his real name), husband and father who chooses to forgive his unfaithful wife so they can rebuild their shattered family. This painful, but beautiful act allows real healing and reconciliation to take place. I worked with them for months and it wasn't easy, but they rebuilt. His deep love provided the fertile soil for the growth of a stronger family. All their kids and his wife benefited from this decision. His grandkids for generations will be blessed by this courageous choice.

Sean, a former addict who, out of his pain, has built a very large and successful food and hot meals program in our community. For over a decade, he and his team have made the choice to serve the most under-resourced in our community. Those living on the streets have hot meals every Friday and families in our community have food on the table because of his sacrificial choice.

Karen, the fifty-plus mom who lost a daughter over two decades ago and gives countless hours of her time to mentor teenage girls. Her choice and compassion have helped provide a place of great healing for many young ladies.

Tony, the mechanic who, after working a full week, volunteers his skills and time and fixes the cars of senior citizens pro bono.

Joe, the combat veteran who suffers from injuries that occurred in battle in Afghanistan, and now serves our Wounded Warriors coming back from the field.

These are all magnificent portraits of the life-transforming power of positive choices.

I guess the Creator could easily have created a life-sustaining world filled with biological robots that had no freedom of choice and simply gave back to Him exactly what He programmed them to. Obviously, He didn't create automatons. It appears that we were given free will so we could exercise the choice to love. The reason I can assume this is because as a father who has "created" two children (to be fair, my wife helped in this process), I can confidently assert that a forced expression of love is not love at all. It seems clear that we were created for relationships and all real relationships have risk. Maybe, just maybe, God designed us this way so we could experience the most profound, moving, and noble expression of choice in relationships — unconditional love. Everything in our soul craves to love and be loved like this, but there lies the risk. We can also use that same power to destroy.

The only way we can understand the life-transforming power of love and compassion is with the backdrop of choice, pain, and suffering. Love and pain are two sides of the same coin, called choice. While we wish for a world without the latter, we would, in the same wish, erase the former.

The Bigger Picture

While poor choices are the source of most of humanity's pain, they are not the *only* source. What about disease, natural disasters, birth defects, and the like? Those are not always the result of human choices, and yet they can cause tremendous difficulty and pain as well.

While it's true that without choice we might be free from much pain, it's also true that we wouldn't know how to love and be loved. If God is an infinite, uncaused, eternal creator, doesn't it stand to reason that our very small perspective is but a glimpse of the timeless whole? I've personally witnessed much beauty emerge from pain and loss. I have been positively shaped by it as well, and am a much better man because of it.

My father's stroke was nobody's choice and left a huge hole in my life that brought about a great deal of pain for many years. But through that pain, I made choices about the kind of man I would become. I'm far from perfect, but it has helped me to be more compassionate and tender. I've focused on helping others work through life's difficulties. My greatest pain became my greatest gift.

The right perspective on the more difficult side of life often brings great compassion, humility, generosity, and empathy. Those qualities make us more fully human. In his wonderful book, *CrossRoads,* William Paul Young beautifully paints this picture better than I could:

> "He [Jack] scanned the room. "Here, let me give you an example." Jack walked to the dresser by the window, on which, among other items, rested a garden pot. In it bloomed a stunning multicolored tulip. He brought it back and sat down. Carefully he began to break away the dirt, gently, so as not to injure the plant, until he revealed the bulb, the stem, and the flower above.
>
> "This is a classical parrot tulip," he explained, "grown right in your own backyard. Notice" — he leaned in so Tony could look closely — "these extraordinary petals. They are feathery and twisted, fringes of scalloped edges that curl around a variety

> of colors, gold and apricot and bluish-purple. Look, there are even ravines of green that run through the yellows. Magnificent!
>
> "Now look here, Tony, at the bulb that produced this wondrous flower. It looks like an old piece of wood or clod of dirt, something that one would discard if one didn't know better. It really is nothing to look at, nothing that would draw your attention, utterly common. This root, Tony..." Jack was animated, now carefully replanting it in the tea-pot, moving and packing the soil with tender care. "This root is the life-before, everything you know and experience, rippled as it is with foretastes of something else, something more. And within what you know and experience, all part of the root, you find hints of the flower — in music and art and story and family and laughter and discovery and innovation and work and presence. But having seen the root only, could you begin to imagine such a wonder as the flower? There will be a moment, Tony, when you finally see the flower, and in that moment, everything about the root will make utter and complete sense."[1]

The problem with pain is that it's a "root" issue. When pain is all we see, we don't realize the beauty that it can produce. And the reason many have such a difficult time accepting that God and pain can reasonably co-exist is because all we are willing to see is the root — that is, this short, material, physical life, with all its problems and pitfalls. But, if God is real, and the evidence suggests that He must be, then all of this life may very well be simply the soil that prepares us for much better—much more.

Pain Produces Beauty

I have personally experienced quite a bit of pain and loss and I've had the honor of walking with many friends through similar losses. I have witnessed firsthand both the bitterness and beauty that can come from such pain. Pat and Janet are wonderful examples of the latter. Their daughter, Rachel, was born with Thanataphoric Dysplasyia, a form of dwarfism. Affected infants die shortly after birth from respiratory failure due to underdeveloped lungs. Surgery couldn't fix her body. Medical interventions couldn't save her life. Pat and Janet were told she might survive one day, two days at best. Doctors told them, "Make the most of your time." They did, for the twenty-five days God allowed Rachel to be on this earth.

What becomes of such pain? In addition to sharing their story on a personal level last year, Janet took her story to the next level and held the first annual "Love and Loss" conference. Women from all over the nation traveled to the Pacific Northwest to grieve and laugh and learn and heal. As I write this chapter, Janet is busy writing a book on the topic as well as planning the second conference. Janet is taking the pain of her loss and planting it as a seed into the lives of other women. From that seed, something beautiful will blossom. As Janet puts it, "Isn't it interesting? The doctors said, "Make the most of your time." God is now allowing me to redeem my time through Love and Loss."

"Foul!" The atheist cries here. We wouldn't have to see all that "beauty" if it weren't for the pain! And what about all the bitterness and anger that also comes from such loss? Wouldn't life be so much better without all the pain? And doesn't that prove that God doesn't exist or, in the least, He doesn't care? To answer the last three questions, no, no, and no.

Pain is not evidence against the existence of God. A painless life is also a loveless life. We have pain because we have choice, and we have love because we have choice. In fact, it's through pain that we see the most beautiful facets of humanity. Rising out of the ashes of life are the best and brightest of our stories. All of our heroes and heroines emerge from pain. The great stories of compassion, nobility, courage, and sacrifice all come through pain. Not only does pain not disprove the arguments for God's existence, it actually strengthens them. Only from pain can we see the best of what we were created to be. Through it, we can most clearly see the love and forgiveness of God. But, at the end of the day, that too is our choice.

Pain and love are two sides of the same coin of choice. We would wish for a life without the former, but in the same wish we would erase the latter.

Our mounting evidence from the previous seven questions proves beyond reasonable doubt that the creator of the universe is:

> **Powerful** — this is obvious from the size and scope of the universe — which came from nothing.
>
> **Spaceless** — because it created space, the supernatural cause must exist outside of space.

Timeless — because it created time, the supernatural cause must exist outside of time.

Independent of creation — this is based on logic and reason. The creator cannot be part of creation that came from nothing. The creator must be outside of and independent of that creation.

Personal—to change a state of absolute nothingness into something requires volition, and volition is a choice. Choices are made by intelligent beings, not by random forces.

Intelligent — The remarkable design of the universe requires a super intelligent being to conceive and construct it. We are clearly talking about a being and not an impersonal force.

Purposed — The well-designed universe isn't just here; it appears designed to produce intelligent life. It has purpose and that stems from a purposeful Designer.

Life-Giver — The gap between living and non-living is beyond words. The power, intelligence, purpose, and design to bring about a living being from non-living matter is supernatural.

Immaterial Mind — Our own conscious awareness apart from our physical body is a solid clue that the creator is a consciously, aware immaterial being.

Moral Law Giver — The overwhelming evidence of the existence of right and wrong, good and evil, is another clue to the character of God. God is a moral being and has woven a moral code into the very fabric of our being.

Given the evidence from pain we can also add:

Healer - Because of the gift of choice, there is undeniable pain in the world. This pain does not at all negate or deny the existence of God. In fact, it is often through pain and loss that we are able to see love, beauty, compassion, and healing.

Chapter Summary

1. Pain, suffering, and loss are very emotional issues and cause many of us to doubt or deny the existence of a "good" god.

2. The majority of pain we experience in life comes from exercising the power of choice. God gave us a free will, like Him, and we often exercise that free will in hurtful ways.

3. Like nuclear power, choices can be used in hurtful or helpful ways.

4. Pain and love are two sides of the same coin. If the choice to cause pain was removed from us, we would also be robbed of the ability to choose love. We were created to love and receive love.

5. Pain caused from natural disasters and disease also doesn't undermine the evidence for God. Because our view is so limited and temporal, we can miss the long-term beauty amidst the short term pain.

6. The greatest stories of heroism, compassion, nobility, sacrifice, and unconditional love blossom out of human pain. That choice gives us a strong glimpse into the eternal heart of God.

Tough Question 8

Do All Religions Lead to God?

Chapter 13

"I am the way, the truth, and the life. No one comes to the Father, but through me."

— Jesus

We've taken the seven previous questions to clearly, methodically, and logically establish beyond a reasonable doubt there is a creator. The evidence from exploring those questions also gives a good picture as to the nature and character of God. Let's review:

> The size, scope, and origin of the universe proves that God is a powerful creator.
>
> The design and fine tuning of the universe shows that God is an intelligent designer.
>
> The complexity of life and biological information shows that God is a life giver.

> Our awareness and introspection are clues that God is a conscious soul.
>
> The moral code demonstrated by every people group everywhere shows that God is a moral being.
>
> The power of choice, and the pain and love that come from it, demonstrates personal free will and compassion.

Let's put those attributes into a coherent sentence.

> *All the scientific, philosophical, and logical evidence we have examined reasonably demonstrate that the universe was intentionally created and designed by a disembodied, eternal, life giving, moral, compassionate being.*

If we're going to explore the world's religions and ask why there are so many and why they're so different, we must keep what we've learned about God in mind. Using that evidence, we will explore which religions, if any, most accurately discuss the God the evidence reveals.

Blind Monks

There's a popular story that is often used to explain how all religions eventually lead to God. Several blind monks are asked to place their hands on an object and describe what they feel. The first blind monk says, "It feels like a large snake." The second disagrees and replies, "Not at all. It feels like a rough wall."

"You two are crazy," states the third. "It's far more like a tree trunk." The fourth one laughs, "Oh, how misguided you all are. I can confidently say that it's a rope." An observer watches the scene unfold and hears the description as each of the blind monks feels a different part of an elephant. The first held the trunk, the second felt the elephant's side, the third wrapped his arms around a leg, and the fourth grabbed the tail. Each is imperfectly describing a part of a much larger whole and arguing with the others over its nature.

This story is often used to describe the nature of religions. The main point of the story is that all religions have a limited understanding of God, and need to recognize that others are holding onto a piece of the much larger truth they are all part of.

At first glance, this analogy has a very earthy wisdom feel to it, and many quickly agree with it and give all religions equal footing. However, it has two fatal flaws and begins to break down under further scrutiny.

> **Fatal Flaw #1:** The observer's vantage point. In the story, there's an outside observer who knows the truth about the monks and the nature of the elephant. The person telling the story always takes the place of this observer. In other words, *they* have

correct sight and *their* view of religions is the correct one. They've placed themselves in the seat of an enlightened, objective observer and knower of truth. They chuckle at the arrogance of each of the blind monk's insistence that he knows the truth while they arrogantly state that they are the ones that can see the whole truth. What gives them the ability to claim such a vantage point? Can you see the double standard here? What I see is irony. The story makes sense if you believe there is an absolute truth, but this story is supposed to be an argument against exactly that.

Fatal Flaw #2: Misunderstanding of religions. In the story, each of the parts of the elephant stands for different but very compatible understandings about God. However, this comparison quickly fails under cross examination. While different parts of an elephant feel different and have different functions, they clearly all "agree" with one another in the making of a whole elephant. The same can't be said of different religions. Some religions, like Buddhism for example, don't include a supreme being at all. Others, like Hinduism, include millions of gods. Those are not compatible. Either God exists or He doesn't. Period. Many religions have incompatible beliefs and they can't all be right.

Pluralism

We live in a very pluralistic society. Pluralism is the belief that a "plurality" of beliefs should be valued and each and every belief system should be treated as valid. Pop culture pressures people to conform to the idea that if you don't validate other people's beliefs, then you are "narrow minded," "hate filled," "dogmatic," or some other label. That pressure encourages the critical thinker to keep her beliefs to herself. The silent statement is that all beliefs have merit, except for the belief that all beliefs don't have merit.

While I strongly agree with the idea of respecting all people and their rights to believe what they choose, I disagree with the notion that all beliefs have equal validity. That is simply a logical fallacy. We have somehow devolved to the point of embracing the notion that to "disagree with" means to disrespect or even hate. That is simply ridiculous. Every one of us is fully capable of loving and respecting those we disagree with.

Every good parent knows this to be true. When my five year-old daughter decided to practice her ABC's with a bolt on the hood of our nice, new black Mazda 323, I strongly disagreed with her belief that it was OK to do so. I still loved her deeply.

There are people who still cling tightly to the belief that the Earth is flat. I respect and value them as people, and I would gladly help them in a time of need, but I can't validate their belief system as legitimate given the evidence. All people have tremendous value, but that doesn't make all world views valid.

Pluralism: a condition or system in which two or more states, groups, principles, sources of authority, etc., coexist.

Many argue that a pluralistic approach is the best way to live, and that adhering to one belief system is exclusive and narrow minded. Think about that. The pluralist says, "My belief system that all belief systems are valid is superior to your view that one belief system is valid and you should adopt my viewpoint." Oh the irony! The pluralist is making the same type of exclusivity statement he accuses the religious of making.

Now we'll take the evidence we have garnered in the previous questions and apply it logically to many worldviews and see what fits the evidence. I will use the terms, "religion," "worldview," "belief system," and "faith system" interchangeably. Everyone has a belief system, a way in which he or she sees the world. Every belief system requires a certain amount of faith, a belief in that which is not seen. The question is simply which belief system most accurately fits the evidence.

Let's begin:

Atheism

Atheism is the belief system that there is no God and there are no supernatural forces. Atheism is often called materialism because of the strongly held belief that only material things are real. Atheists bristle at being labeled a faith system, but their faith is obvious. The atheist has to believe, by faith, that the universe sprang into existence uncaused (unless said atheist claims to have been there to see it. Then we have another situation on our hands.) The atheist has to believe, by faith, that the incredible complexity of the universe, the fine tuning, just happened to come about by chaotic natural forces. The atheist has to believe, by faith, that life sprang up out of non-living chemicals with no intelligent involvement. The atheist has to believe, by faith, that morality and awareness simply evolved over time, even though both run counter to what evolution promotes. As you can see, the atheist has a great deal of faith.

Atheism is most certainly a religion. It is the most popular humanistic religion of our times. It has its prophets: Darwin, Sagan, and Dawkins. It has its creed, "Survival of the fittest." It has its sacred texts, including Darwin's groundbreaking work on evolution and Dawkins's, *The God Delusion.*

While only about five percent of Americans subscribe to the atheistic worldview, they happen to be among the most influential in our nation as teachers and professors. While they have a strong influence, what they're lacking is evidence. In a surprising turn of events, the scientific and logical evidence atheists relied on so heavily one hundred years ago is now completely turning on them and pointing to an uncaused, timeless, intelligent personal creator. As we clearly saw in the previous chapters, atheism is simply an illogical and unreasonable faith system and worldview.

Humanism

One of the arguments aimed at religion is its divisive and even sometimes violent nature. Some believe that religion should be banned, minimized, or relegated to personal belief and not at all allowed into the public discussion. The "history" of religion's divisive nature is often brought up as a reason for such thinking. Let's forget for a moment the absurd nature of such a stance— "My irreligious foundation for my truth claims about how the world works is superior to your religious truth claims about how the world works," and let me state that, to some degree, I agree.

This may surprise you, given that my journey led me to become a full time Christian minister.

I agree that religious views, well, all views, can be divisive in nature. Let's face it, any time we make a truth claim, no matter its basis, it has a divisive potential. Many adherents to religious ideals over the centuries have acted with self-righteousness, greed, violence, arrogance, abuse, and even murder. Those who would like to relegate those behaviors exclusively to religion are willfully ignorant of history. Enter Humanism.

Humanism: an outlook or system of thought attaching prime importance to human, rather than divine or supernatural, matters. Humanist beliefs stress the potential value and goodness of human beings, emphasize common human needs, and seek solely rational ways of solving human problems.

Humanism is nothing more than atheism organized into a movement with the goal of elevating the common good and celebrating the best in humanity. Humanity becomes its own god and achievement the greatest goal. But those lofty goals actually become the most murderous, violent, divisive, and ruthless regimes in human history.

Stalin, Mao, & Hitler

Joseph Stalin, Mao Tse Tung (Mao Zedong), and Adolf Hitler each took over their respective nations with idealistic goals that included eradicating religion and elevating humanism. Stalin and Mao both took their communist and socialist ideas from Karl Marx. Hitler's personal views come from a variety of places including, as we already learned, the works of Charles Darwin.

Regardless of the specific brand of humanism under discussion, the general foundation is clear—humans are their own highest good. What were the results of these noble ideals?

Stalin's brutal regime killed over twenty million of his own countrymen in the totalitarian expression of his ideals.

Hitler's passionate elevation of the Aryan race led to the burning of religious books, the destruction of churches, and the murder of pastors in his own country. His continued zeal led to the genocide of six million Jews and the murder of six million others.

More than Hitler's and Stalin's combined is the mind boggling number killed by the regime of Mao. Through systematic torture, starvation, and violent slaughter the Mao regime killed more than forty-five million Chinese.

Just these three atheist/humanist idealists alone are responsible for the death of roughly seventy-seven million people. All in one century! Contrast that with the Crusades. The Crusades lasted for almost two hundred years and were bloody battles between Islamic and Christian armies for the capital of Jerusalem. In those two hundred years, roughly two hundred thousand people were killed.

Humanism, not religion, is by far the most divisive, murderous, and violent worldview humanity has ever experienced.

Agnosticism

While the atheist confidently asserts, "There is no God," the agnostic's position is, "I'm not sure if there is a God or whether we can even know if there is a God." This person takes a step away from atheism and grants at least the possibility of the existence of God.

There are two types of agnostics, the "arms crossed" agnostic and the "shoulder shrugging" agnostic. The "arms crossed" agnostic takes a firm antagonistic stance and asserts confidently that God cannot be known. This is stated as a truth and a fact. The obvious response is, "How do you know that God can't be known to be true?" This position of skepticism is self-defeating because at some point, the skepticism must turn on itself. Ardent skeptics must be skeptical of their own skepticism.

Agnosticism: is the view that the true values of certain claims—especially claims about the existence or non-existence of God, as well as other religious and metaphysical claims—are unknown or unknowable.

This, more often than not, leads to the "shoulder shrugging" type of agnosticism. Their position is much softer than the hard core agnostic. "I'm not really sure if one can know if there is a God or not," they say as they shrug their shoulders. I have found that this type of person is at least willing to look at the evidence we examined in the preceding chapters to help them gain knowledge and develop the basis to make a reasoned decision.

Pantheism

"Pan" is the Greek word for Earth and "theism" comes from the Greek word for God. Combine the two and you have a word that means "The Earth is God." This worldview is the belief that everything comprises an all-encompassing, immanent god, or that the universe (or nature) is identical with divinity.

Paul Harrison writes,

> *"When we say that the cosmos is divine, we mean it with just as much conviction and emotion as believers say that their god is God. But we are not making a metaphysical statement that is beyond proof or disproof. We are making an ethical statement that means no more, and no less, than this: We should relate to the universe in the same way as believers in God relate to God. That is, with humility, awe, reverence, celebration, and the search for deeper understanding." ("Divine Cosmos, Sacred Earth," from Harrison's Scientific Pantheism website.)*

We see this worldview in many of the "new age" religions of today, as well as many of the tribal and "animistic" people groups around the world. In this belief system, the universe *is* god and this "life force" pervades or animates every tree, animal, stream—everything. This religious view was brought back into pop culture through the most popular movie in cinematic history, Avatar. In James Cameron's blockbuster, the Na'vi tribe worships and is "connected" to Eywa, the spiritual force that guides everything on their planet. Many North American and African tribal peoples embrace a very similar faith. They believe that all living things are connected to a much greater "life force." Buddhism and Taoism

Pantheism: is the belief that the universe (or nature as the totality of everything) is identical with divinity, or that everything composes an all-encompassing, immanent god.

carry similar themes. We will look at Buddhism specifically later in this chapter.

This worldview sounds very wonderful, mystical, and almost magical, but the problem is that this religion simply doesn't fit the evidence and can't reasonably be true. Let's look at that evidence.

Remember the second question we asked about the beginning and nature of the universe, "Why is there something rather than nothing?" An enormous amount of scientific, philosophical, and logical evidence shows that the entire universe and everything in it had a specific beginning point. Out of absolutely nothing, the universe sprang to existence. This is commonly known as the "Big Bang," and scientists refer to this beginning point as the singularity. In that chapter, we discovered the airtight reasoning of the Kalam Cosmological argument. As a review, below are the two premises and the conclusion:

1. Everything that begins to exist must have a cause outside of itself.
   There is simply no such thing as an uncaused beginning.
2. The universe began to exist.
   Remember the evidence from B.E.G.I.N. that we explored, which proves beyond a shadow of a doubt that the universe is not eternal and had a specific beginning point. Anyone who claims that the universe is eternal immediately has serious credibility problems.
3. Therefore, the universe had a cause outside of itself.

This is very important to understand, because pantheism ties deity and divinity to the material universe. That's simply not reasonable, logical, or possible, since the material universe, and everything in it, hasn't always existed and couldn't have created itself. The pantheistic "god" couldn't have created the universe and *be* the universe at the same time. The evidence from creation logically proves that the creator must have existed outside of and apart from creation.

The universe is amazing, beautiful, and awe inspiring, but it's certainly not, can't be, God. The spectacular beauty and wonder that come from the universe are attributed to its incredible design, not its divinity.

Karma

While karma is not, in itself, a religion, I thought it would be good to discuss it because of the place it takes in several religions as well as modern day society and even pop culture. In general, karma is the cosmic law of cause and effect. If one leads a good and helpful life, then this power will reward that person with good outcomes both in this life and in the life to come. The goal, then, is to do good deeds so that you will have good karma and good blessings. This is the major "force" in the Hindu, Buddhist, Jain, and Sikh religions. Karma is not punishment or retribution, but simply an extended expression or consequence of natural acts. Karma means "deed" or "act" and more broadly names the universal principle of cause and effect, action and reaction, that governs all life. The

Karma means action, work, or deed; it also refers to the principle of causality, where intent and actions of an individual influence the future of that individual.

effects experienced also can be mitigated by actions and are not necessarily fated. That is to say, a particular action now is not binding to some particular, pre-determined future experience or reaction; it's not a simple, one-to-one correspondence of reward or punishment. Many Hindus see a god's direct involvement in this process, but more often than not, karma is seen simply as a powerful, invisible cause and effect force. Much as gravity is to the natural world, karma is to the spiritual world—an impersonal force.

Karma was even the "star" of a hit TV show. "My Name is Earl" (2005-2009) was the humorous story of a former derelict who was spending all his time trying to right all his past wrongs and bring good karma back into his life. Virtually every episode had this discussion of the balance of good and bad karma.

MTV is currently running a show entitled "Ridiculousness" where skateboard star turned businessman turned TV host Rob Dyrdek shows clips of homemade videos, usually involving stupidity and pain. One of their recurring categories of clips is "Instant Karma," where an attempted practical joke backfires on the jokester. It's very funny and shows how deeply the idea of karma pervades pop culture.

Why bring karma up? Simple. It doesn't fit the evidence.

The overwhelming evidence shows us that the creator is an intelligent, creative, personal, rational, and conscious mind. Karma, in most belief systems, is an impersonal, unconscious force.

A belief system that has at its core a mindless force rather than an intelligent mind doesn't fit the vast evidence stream.

Polytheism

"Poly" comes from the Greek for many, and theism means God. Polytheism simply means "many gods." There are many belief systems that have polytheism at their core. Many of the Bronze Age and Iron Age powers, like the Egyptians, were polytheists. Ra was the sun god and most powerful of all gods. Osiris was the god of the underworld. Isis was the goddess of marriage and magic. There were many more. Over two dozen gods and goddesses ruled the universe in the belief system of ancient Egypt.

Polytheism is the belief system of classical antiquity. The Romans and Greeks each had their pantheon of gods and goddesses that ruled various parts of the heavens, the Earth, and even Hades. Many of us learned about Zeus, Apollo, Mars, Aphrodite, and the rest of the Greco-Roman cast of deities in literature class.

Modern day polytheistic religions include Shintoism and the most well-known, Hinduism, with over 300 million gods.

It's very difficult to draw a clean line between pantheism (discussed above) and polytheism. Many polytheistic beliefs have the deities linked to nature itself. As we discussed, this simply does not fit the evidence.

Polytheism refers to the worship of, or belief in, multiple deities, usually assembled into a pantheon of gods and goddesses, along with their own religions and rituals.

But what about the polytheistic gods that are not linked to the material universe? Is there anything that precludes the thinking that a plurality of uncaused, timeless, creative, moral, compassionate deities brought the entire universe into existence out of absolutely nothing? In short, no. Enter Occam's Razor. "Occam's what?" you ask.

Occam's Razor, sometimes written as "Ockham's Razor," is the principle that economy, or succinctness, be used in logic and problem-solving. It states that among competing hypotheses, the one that makes the fewest assumptions should be selected.

William of Ockham (c. 1285–1349) is remembered as an influential medieval philosopher and nominalist, though his popular fame as a great logician rests chiefly on the maxim attributed to him and known as Ockham's Razor. The term "razor" refers to distinguishing between two hypotheses either by "shaving away" unnecessary assumptions or cutting apart two similar conclusions. The term "Occam's Razor" was first used in 1852 in the works of Sir William Hamilton. Ockham himself did not invent his "razor," but it's named for him because of how often he used its logical premise.

This sharp use of logic (pun clearly intended) did not originate with Ockham and can be traced through the centuries. Maimonides, Ptolemy, Aristotle, and Saint Thomas Aquinas all advocated for the cutting away of a complicated theory when a simpler, reasonable one will suffice.

I mention Saint Thomas Aquinas because he uses Occam's Razor in the same way we'll apply it here. In his *Summa Theologica* (1225-1274), he states that "It is superfluous to suppose that what can be accounted for by a few principles has been produced by many." He goes on to argue for the existence of one creator.

Occam's Razor is not relegated to philosophical debates about the nature of the universe. All detectives use a form of this logic in problem solving. If a bank has been robbed, there's no reason to look for multiple suspects if all the evidence points to a one person job. It would be unreasonable to look for a team unless the evidence suggests it.

There's no need to believe in many uncaused, powerful, timeless, intelligent, creative, moral creators when *one* uncaused, powerful, timeless, intelligent, creative, moral creator is sufficient enough to fully explain the evidence we see.

That leads us to discuss what the evidence does suggest.

Monotheism

All the scientific, philosophical, and moral evidence leads to the reasonable conclusion that there is one God responsible for the existence and design of the universe. Monotheism, as you might have guessed, comes from "mono" for one and "theism" — God. Monotheism is the belief in one God. All other faith systems, natural or supernatural in origin, just don't have the credible evidence that monotheism does.

There are three well-known monotheistic religions in the world: Judaism, Christianity, and Islam. The last two, Christianity and Islam, account for roughly 3.5 billion of the world's 7 billion people. All three find their monotheistic roots in the Bible and the patriarch, Abraham, is recognized as the father of all three. Judaism and Islam diverge with Abraham's sons — Isaac, the Father of the Hebrew tribes, and Ishmael, the Father of the Muslim tribes. Christianity differs from both of them based on the identity and work of Jesus.

Monotheism: belief in the existence of one god, or in the oneness of God; as such, it is distinguished from polytheism, the belief in the existence of many gods.

history. In His time, He was seen as an irritant, healer, troublemaker, revolutionary, savior, criminal, and king. His identity and claims have been debated for over two millennia, and He is still a point of contention to this day. At a dinner party or other social gathering, you'd scarcely raise an eyebrow by talking about Hinduism, Buddhism, Agnosticism, or basically any other worldview, but talk about Jesus...show stopper.

Because of Jesus' outrageous claims and the movement He began, we'll focus our final question on Him. Either He is God Himself and His words need to be heeded, or He is a total fraud. If He's a charlatan or the stories about Him are untrue, then we can look elsewhere for more clues about the further identification of God. We can examine the evidence and either embrace Him or reject Him. What we can't do, however, is ignore Him.

Chapter Summary

1. All people have value and worth, but not all beliefs are equally valid when considering the evidence.
2. Truth doesn't change based on a person's opinion. The Earth isn't flat for some and a sphere for others.
3. The evidence for God shows that atheistic religions like humanism, Buddhism, and materialism have no foundation.
4. Logic and reason show that God can't *be* the universe and have created the universe. This rules out pantheistic religions.
5. Occam's Razor rules out all polytheistic religions. The evidence doesn't show the need for multiple gods.
6. The simplest answer for the evidence we see for God is monotheism. A single, powerful, intelligent, uncaused, timeless being created everything.
7. There are three major monotheistic religions: Islam, Judaism, and Christianity.

Question 9

Is Jesus Really God?

Chapter 14

"If you have seen the Father you have seen me. I and the Father are one."

Jesus

Jesus. His name is the most controversial in history. It's far easier to talk about politics, the economy, religion in general, or the effect of pop culture on our youth. Just mention the name Jesus and take cover. To some, Jesus is the Son of God, the anointed, the Christ —born to a virgin more than 2,000 years ago. To others, Jesus was just a man, though a very influential one, who ignited a revolution and spawned many moral streams now incorporated into modern day Christianity. Finally, to others, Jesus is little more than a myth — like Robin Hood. They maintain he was elevated to legend status by Paul and the disciples, who needed his impact to propagate their churches.

The Crusades were fought in his name. Thousands of hospitals, orphanages, soup kitchens and homeless shelters have been built to carry out his teachings.

Like I said, controversial.

But is Jesus much more than just a historical figure? All of Christianity, indeed, all of humanity, rests on one question — was Jesus divine? Was he God? Did he, in fact, rise from the dead to cover our sins?

If he didn't, then we will need to continue our search for the religion or religions that best describes and reveals the creator that our previous evidence points to. If Jesus really was who he claimed to be, then our search is over and we can settle in to deciding what to do about what we've learned.

Powerful evidences suggest His story is true.

Before we can tackle the question, "Is Jesus Really God?" it's only logical that we answer the question, "Did Jesus Really Live?"

Did Jesus Really Live?

Many people are under the false impression that the only documentation of Jesus's life is the Christian Bible. Operating under that misconception, they then reason that since the Bible declares both itself and Jesus to be divinely inspired, it cannot really be trusted.

The Bible is not the only historical voice about Jesus. There are many other voices that *agree* with what the Bible says about the historical Jesus. Let's see what they have to say.

One of the most important historians of the ancient world is Flavius Josephus (ca. 37 – ca. 100)

Josephus was born just after Jesus was killed and lived in the Galilean region where much of Jesus's ministry took place. Josephus was, at one time, a revolutionary against Rome because of their oppression of the Jews, but through a series of fortunate events, he lived out the second half of his life in Rome, serving as a historian under the Emperor Domitian. One of his greatest works, and probably most known, is his *Antiquities of the Jews*, which he finished around A.D. 93. Though Josephus was not a Christian, he wrote about Jesus:

> *"At this time [of Pilate] there was a wise man who was called Jesus. His conduct was good and (he) was known to be virtuous. And many people from among the Jews and the other nations became his disciples. Pilate condemned him to be crucified and to die. Both those who had become his disciples did not abandon his discipleship. They reported that he had appeared to them three days after his crucifixion, and that he was alive; accordingly he was perhaps the Messiah, concerning whom the prophets have recounted wonders."* [1]

Josephus didn't mention only Jesus, he also recorded historical events from the life of the early church that Jesus's followers started.

> *"Festus was now dead, and Albinus was but upon the road, so he (Ananus the high priest of the of the Jews) assembled the Sanhedrin of the judges, and brought before them the brother of Jesus, who was called the Christ, whose name was James, and some others, and when he had formed an accusation against them as breakers of the law, he delivered them to be stoned."* [2]

Here we have two powerful references to Jesus by one of the most respected historians of the ancient world.

Are there other historians that mention Jesus as a historical figure? The answer is a resounding yes. In fact, in addition to Josephus, there are nine other known non-Christian sources who mention Jesus within 150 years of his life. [3] You may think that ten references to Jesus doesn't sound like much, considering his impact. Remember, this is the ancient world, and then consider this fact: Over the same 150 years, there are nine non-Christian sources who mention Tiberius Caesar, the Roman Emperor at the time of Jesus.[4] If you take away all the Christian sources that speak of Jesus, he's still mentioned more often by historians than the contemporary emperor of Rome. If you include Christian sources, then historians mentioning Jesus outnumber those mentioning Tiberius forty-three to ten. More than four to one! [5]

A full discussion of the historicity of Jesus' life is outside the scope of this book. For those who want a greater study on that, I'd recommend *The Case for the Resurrection of Jesus*. Habermas and Licona do an exceptional job and their book is probably the premier study on the historicity of the resurrection of Jesus.

For those who want to reject the historically documented fact that Jesus was a real person, if they want to remain intellectually credible, they would have to dismiss the existence of Tiberius Caesar, the Emperor of Rome!

What do we know of Jesus from these non-Christian (and several are anti-Christian) historical documents?

1. Jesus obviously lived during the time of Tiberius Caesar.
2. He was known as a "virtuous" person.
3. His reputation was as a "wonder worker."
4. Many thought he was the Messiah.

5. He was crucified under the leadership of Pontius Pilate.
6. He was crucified during the Passover celebration.
7. His disciples believed he rose from the dead.
8. His disciples were willing to die for that belief.
9. He had a brother named James.
10. Christianity spread all the way to Rome within fifty years after Jesus' death.[6]

For those who want to reject the historically documented fact that Jesus was a real person, if they want to remain intellectually credible, they would have to dismiss the existence of Tiberius Caesar, the Emperor of Rome!

These documented facts are congruent with what the New Testament record reveals at each point. This is a very important discovery. While non-Christian historians may not agree that Jesus was divine, it can't be rationally argued that he didn't exist. The non-Christian and Christian records about Jesus agree at each point where they share the same details. It's then very unreasonable to believe that Jesus is anything other than a historical figure. How could all these different writers agree on a story line that supports the Biblical record? The obvious answer is that they are each reporting historical facts about a real person of influence.

Now that we have clearly established that Jesus was, in fact, a historical reality confirmed by multiple non-Christian sources, it's time to turn to the most well-known accounts about the life of Jesus — the New Testament.

Is the New Testament Trustworthy?

There is no doubt that the most important historical documentation about Jesus comes from the Christian New Testament. Like every other historical document, the New Testament needs to be checked for both authenticity and veracity. Is the documentation we have reliable, and does it speak the truth?

Do We Have Reliable Documentation?

There are several misconceptions about the New Testament. One of those big misconceptions is that it is a single document written by a single individual. This misconception came up recently in a discussion I was having with an agnostic on the subject of Jesus. He said, "I could write a realistic fictional account of a person and bury it in a jar to be found 2,000 years later and many might believe it's true as well." I've heard quite a few similar statements over the years. The documentation of the life of Jesus is nothing like that. It is *not* one person writing one document. The New Testament is actually twenty-seven different documents written at twenty-seven different times by nine different authors from different locations over roughly a forty year span. These twenty-seven documents were then spread around the world and copied thousands of times, retelling, again and again, their incredible story. It's this wealth of historical documentation that builds the strong foundation for the reliability of the New Testament records about Jesus.

In a class I regularly teach on this subject, I like to compare the historicity of the New Testament with other well-known historical writings. It always shocks my listeners how the New Testament favorably compares. Let's do that comparison here.

The Manuscript Showdown [7]

Plato

Have you ever heard of Plato? Of course you have. Plato was the brilliant Greek scholar and philosopher who founded The Academy in Athens. The Academy was the first institution of higher learning in the Western world. He was a student of Socrates and is credited as one of the most influential thinkers in history. With such an impressive resume, how many known documents would you think form the basis of all we know about Plato's teachings? The answer might surprise you. All we know about Plato comes from….seven documents. Seven! Even more shocking is that the earliest of those manuscripts is dated roughly 1,200 years after Plato wrote them. Please let that sink in. There were only seven copies, and there was well over 1,000 years from his originals to our earliest copies. With such little manuscript evidence, it's surprising that we never hear people debating whether Plato lived or that what he said was passed on accurately.

Aristotle

Aristotle was Plato's most brilliant student and left an impressive legacy of his own. He joined Plato's academy in Athens at age eighteen and stayed for nineteen years. He tutored Alexander the Great for over thirty years and his impact on one of the greatest leaders in history is impossible to calculate. He wrote extensively on a variety of subjects, from biology, zoology, physics, logic and philosophy. After Plato died, Aristotle's focus shifted from Platonism toward a more scientific empiricism. Aristotle is considered the first true scientist in history. His influence on ethics and classical logic is still felt today. With all of this incredible influence, you would think Aristotle's manuscript evidence would be extensive. Though it's more than what we have from his mentor, we still only have forty-nine copies. Like Plato, the amount of time from his writing to his earliest copies is significant—1,400 years. Yet again, I've never heard a single college professor question the authenticity or reliability of his works.

Homer

I could talk about many other famous writers of antiquity, but the manuscript evidence by comparison is so paltry as to embarrass them. So let's jump to the second most documented work in history — the *Iliad*.

I remember having to read Homer's *Iliad* in CP English. There I sat in Mrs. McAdam's class, wondering why I had to study a 3,000 year old fictional story about a warrior named Achilles and the destruction of Troy. I do have to admit, the Trojan horse deception was quite brilliant though. I asked myself many questions about the story. How big *was* that Trojan horse? Was Achilles as buff as he sounds? How would Helen compare to the gorgeous supermodels of our day? But what I never asked was, "Did Homer really write this?" It was never brought up, debated, or even addressed. It was presented as fact that this was written by Homer, so we studied it and regurgitated it for a test.

As it turns out, this classic work by Homer is the silver medalist for manuscript quantity with 643 copies. [7] Compared to Plato's seven or Caesar's ten or Aristotle's forty-nine, that's a large amount. However, compared to the grand champion of manuscript evidence, it compares quite poorly. Let's now look at the New Testament.

New Testament Manuscripts[7]

There are over 5,500 hand-written Greek manuscripts of the New Testament. In addition to these, there are more than 9,000 manuscripts which were written in different languages as the New Testament story spread throughout the ancient world. These Latin, Arabic, Coptic, and Syriac manuscripts provide an enormous foundation for the historical evidence of the New Testament's reliability. If you combine all these manuscripts, there are nearly 15,000 complete texts, large sections, or partial fragments. This is an overwhelming amount of evidence. As we learned, Homer's Iliad comes in at number two with only 643 manuscripts. Most ancient works whose authenticity we take for granted have become popular based on fewer than a dozen manuscripts. Interestingly, few people question the historical reliability of those works even though, by comparison, their manuscript evidence is so anemic.

If this were a boxing match, it would be a first round knockout.

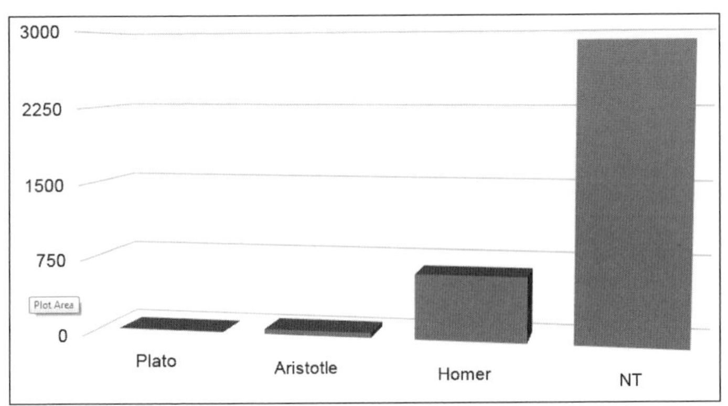

Number of Manuscripts

Dating [7]

The number of manuscripts isn't the only qualifier historians look for when determining a manuscript's reliability. Dating is also an important factor. The two most important numbers in dating are the year of the earliest manuscript copy we possess (since there are no originals of any of these works) and the gap between the time the manuscript was originally written and that date.

Author	Date Written	Earliest Copy	Time Span	# of Copies
Plato	427-347 BC	900 AD	1200 years	7
Aristotle	384-322 BC	1100 AD	1400 years	49
Homer	900 BC	400 BC	500 years	643
NT	40-100 AD	125 AD	25 years	29,000+

Let's go back to Plato. Plato died in 347 B.C. The earliest manuscript we have of his works — and remember, we only have seven of them — isn't dated until around 850 A.D. This leaves us with a time gap of roughly 1,200 years. That's a very large time span. Imagine if the only manuscripts we had on the history of the United States of America were copies written *a thousand years from now!* That's roughly 1,200 years after our nation was founded. How much trust would you put in such documentation? And yet, no one really questions the authenticity of Plato's work.

Homer's *Iliad* fares much better that Plato. Homer lived around 900 B.C. and the earliest copy of his most famous work shows up around 500 years later. That is pretty good by most standards for ancient documents, especially when you remember that we have 643 copies. But once again, when stacked up against the New Testament, there really is no comparison.

The New Testament not only has, by far, the *most* copies; it also has the *earliest* copies. The earliest undisputed piece of the New Testament is called the John Rylands fragment (so named because it rests in his library in Manchester, England). It was discovered in the Egyptian market in 1920. It's a piece of John's eyewitness testimony, John 18:31-33, 37-38. This fragment is dated between A.D. 117-138. This is roughly only twenty-five years after John's gospel was written. Since it was found in Egypt, it also shows how far the gospel accounts traveled in such a short time span. This is a staggering realization.

We have manuscripts of complete New Testament books that have a time gap of only 150 years. We have almost complete New Testament manuscripts, including *all* of the eyewitness accounts, that are only 200 years removed from the originals. The famous Codex Vaticanus, an entire New Testament manuscript, survives from 325 A.D., giving us a time span of less than 300 years. The graph below shows the manuscript gap comparison of ancient documents.

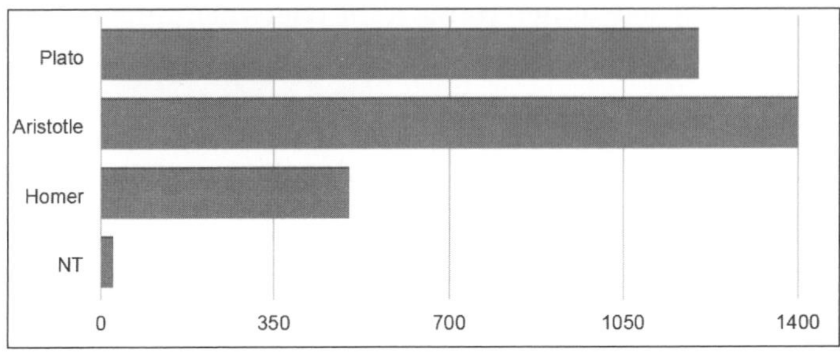

Time Span Between Authorship and Earliest Document

An overall comparison of both quantity and dating of famous manuscripts looks like this. As far as manuscript evidence, there really is no comparison.

An unbiased observer must come to the conclusion that the New Testament has, by far, the most support of any writings from the ancient world. However, that is not the only question we need to ask about the New Testament. It is one thing to have vast amounts of documentation supporting a manuscript's historical position. That speaks to its reliability. It's quite another thing to know if its content is truthful. That speaks to its veracity. So how do we know that what the New Testament, specifically the gospels, says about Jesus is true?

Do We Have Truthful Documentation?

The New Testament was not written as a religious document. It was written as a history of real life events. We can then examine it under the same light and with the same approach as other historical documents. We can ask the same questions that would be asked of other writings. Do we know the author? Can he be trusted? How well received was the writing in its own time? Does what's written line up with other facts we know to be true? These questions will help us determine if the overwhelming documentation about the historical Jesus can also help us learn if he was more than just a teacher or prophet. We already know that Jesus was a real person, but was He more? Are the accounts of His life and resurrection true? With that in mind, let's take a closer look at the eyewitness testimony and determine if the resurrection was a historical reality.

The Followers — Matthew, John, Peter

Much of the New Testament and two of the four gospels were written by eyewitnesses to the life, death, and resurrection of Jesus. Remember, we have thousands and thousands of documents that share their stories, far more than any other document from the ancient world. The weight of their story must be taken into account. Let's meet these men and see what they have to say.

Matthew

Matthew was a tax collector with a booth on the Sea of Galilee. To understand his story, we must understand how much tax collectors were despised. Our own I.R.S. agents are not likely to be invited to many birthday parties, but the tax collectors of first century Galilee were absolutely hated. The nation of Israel was occupied under the control and oppression of Rome. Like any government, Rome needed to collect taxes to fund its operation. Of course, they didn't have the electronic and mail systems we do now. They had to rely on face-to-face collections. The Roman government would auction off the right to collect taxes to wealthy Roman citizens, who would then hire locals to do the actual collecting. At each level of this pyramid scheme, the person could collect as much as possible (keeping the difference) while simply passing the required amount up the chain. Tax collecting was a very lucrative business. The front line locals, like Matthew, were despised for two reasons. First, they were known for gouging the hard-working people of their community so they could become wealthy. Second, and more importantly, they aided the Roman nation — their oppressors. They were traitors. Imagine what you'd think about the twenty-something dropout who's selling drugs to junior-high students behind the gym after school. Despicable!

And yet, despite Matthew's reputation as a tax collector, Jesus, the traveling teacher, invites him to join Him as a disciple. We can imagine what the other followers thought of that invitation! Matthew later left his business, his lucrative lifestyle, and his only means of support behind to follow this Rabbi. He spent the next three years as an eyewitness to the life and teachings of Jesus. It's very clear from Matthew's account that he is writing history. From the events surrounding Jesus's birth, to the journey of the Magi, the ministry of John the Baptist, and through the recounting of Jesus's ministry, Matthew writes of actual, historical events. It's because of Matthew that we have the great "Sermon on the Mount." After Jesus's death, it's Matthew who describes the discovery of the open tomb by the women, as well as the empty tomb cover-up story fabricated by the Roman supervisors. As we proceed through these accounts, we'll ask, "What would motivate Matthew to write these things down if they were not true?"

Imagine how you might feel about the twenty-one year old high school dropout selling meth to junior high kids. That's how Jesus' culture felt about tax collectors.

Of course, Matthew isn't the only voice speaking of such events. If that were so, it would be easy to dismiss Jesus as nothing more than just a historical figure. In fact, He is much more.

John

John, who, like Matthew, became a follower of Jesus and an eyewitness to the events of His ministry, first met Jesus while at work. John was a fisherman. Along with his brother James and their cousins Peter and Andrew, he ran a small fishing company under the guidance of their father, Zebedee. Upon hearing Jesus's teachings, they decided to join His small, but growing, band of disciples. They left the family business and the security it provided and traveled with Jesus as his followers. John gives us a very different perspective about Jesus's life than Matthew does. While the two eyewitness accounts document Jesus's ministry from a different point of view, they agree on the historical facts. Namely, Jesus was falsely accused by the Jews, crucified by the Romans, the empty tomb was discovered by a female after three days, and Jesus rose again in a bodily fashion. Why document these things unless they were true? John didn't write only his gospel account of Jesus. Four other books in the New Testament bear his authorship. And almost as though he could foresee the skepticism that would later come about the reality of Jesus's life, he wrote, *"We proclaim to you the one who existed from the beginning, whom we have heard and seen. We saw him with our own eyes and touched him with our own hands. He is the Word of life. We proclaim to you what we ourselves have actually seen and heard."* 1 John 1:1, 3

Peter

As mentioned, Peter, James, John, and Peter's brother Andrew, all fishermen, joined Jesus's traveling ministry. While we have no gospel account of Jesus's ministry from Peter, he most certainly left his mark on much of the documentation we have about Jesus. He was interviewed by both Mark and Luke (whom we will meet in a bit) for their historical accounts about Jesus. In addition to that, Peter wrote two letters about Jesus to local churches that are now included in our documentation about

Jesus. In one of those letters to a local church, he clearly agrees with John's eyewitness account, *"For we did not follow cleverly devised stories when we told you about the coming of our Lord Jesus Christ in power, but we were eyewitnesses of his majesty."* 2 Peter 1:16

The Historian — Luke

Luke is the only gentile — non Jewish — author in the entire Bible. Luke is a physician turned researcher, and becomes one of the greatest historians from the ancient world. Through the course of his research, he becomes a Christ-follower and decides to leave the world with an accurate account of the life of Christ and the birth of the early church. He begins his gospel account with his motivation for his writing,

> *"Many have undertaken to draw up an account of the things that have been fulfilled among us, just as they were handed down to us by those who from the first were eyewitnesses and servants of the word. With this in mind, since I myself have carefully investigated everything from the beginning, I too decided to write an orderly account for you, most excellent Theophilus, so that you may know the certainty of the things you have been taught." Luke 1: 1 - 4*

From those opening lines in his letter to his friend, Theophilus, Luke carefully documents the main events in the ministry, death, and resurrection of Jesus. His research confirms what the eyewitnesses themselves said about Jesus. This gives us another layer of confirmation as to both the work and the identity of Jesus.

"Hold on a second," the skeptic says, "Why should I believe these guys? They all became followers." We'll address the questions of the modern day skeptic later. For now, we will move from Jesus's disciples to a couple writers who were not.

Luke is a lot like me and many who might read this book. He was a skeptic who was drawn to the Jesus story through questions and research. The evidence led him to become a follower.

The Skeptic — James

What would it take for you to believe that your older brother was God Himself? This was the position of James, Jesus's next younger brother. We are told that Jesus had four younger brothers, half brothers to be exact, and at least two sisters. His brothers, James (not the James who was a fisherman turned disciple) and Jude both documented the teachings of Jesus. James, however, was a hard sell and for a long time did not believe Jesus was the Messiah. John writes, "For even his own brothers did not believe in him." John 7:5 In fact, James, along with the rest of his family, thought his older brother was a bit — crazy. Mark documents this, saying, "When his family heard about this, they went *to take charge of him, for they said, "He is out of his mind."* Mark 3:21

For Jesus's entire ministry, James was not a believer and was even embarrassed by his older brother. How is it then, that just a few years after Jesus's death we see this same brother as the leader of the Jerusalem church? What

Point to Ponder

How would you react if your older brother claimed to be the Savior of the world?

changed that James wrote a letter to a local church proclaiming, *"James, a servant of God and of the Lord Jesus Christ."*? James 1:1

What sort of event would cause a person to make such a dramatic shift? James went from thinking his older brother was insane to publicly proclaiming Him as *"Lord"* and *"Christ."* It would take a monumental event indeed for such a change — a resurrection, perhaps?

The Hunter — Paul

Even more dramatic than James's transformation is the incredible story of Paul. While James was a skeptic, Paul was an outright enemy. Unlike all the people we've met so far, Paul did not know Jesus during His ministry. He met him later. Paul, who we first meet as Saul, comes into the New Testament record as an opponent to the growing new church. As a powerful, devout Jewish religious leader, he is morally opposed to this sect that he considers heretical. Luke's research shows that Saul oversaw the stoning death of the Christ-follower Stephen and was then given the legal authority to hunt down and jail other Christ-followers on behalf of the Jewish leadership. Then something miraculous happened, and afterwards, Saul changed his name to Paul and went on to be the greatest church planter of his generation. He embarked on three or four dangerous voyages, risking his life on each one to tell of Jesus as a risen Savior. He was ridiculed, beaten, jailed, stoned, shipwrecked, and eventually killed for his faith. He ended up writing nearly half the books in the New Testament and became one of the most influential Christ followers in human history. What in the world could spark such a change?

On one of those seek-and-destroy-Christ-follower missions, Saul had a remarkable encounter with Jesus. The very one he called a myth, and his followers heretic, met him personally in a very dramatic way. It would be tough to continue business as usual after such a meeting. That encounter not only changed Saul, it changed history.

Imagine the high priest of the KKK becoming the most ardent and passionate spokesman for civil rights. That is the level of transformation in Paul. Something very powerful sparked that change.

The Women

In the modern American courtroom, when a lawyer is trying to substantiate her case, she puts credible witnesses on the stand. Witnesses whose accounts are trustworthy or whose expertise in their field is strong enough to sway a jury. No good lawyer is going to bring to the stand a witness whose history or lifestyle brings doubt to the mind of the juror.

That brings us to the eyewitness testimony of the women in the Jesus story. It's hard for the modern reader to grasp how strange it was for a first century writer to include women as central figures in the testimony about the resurrection of Jesus and the empty tomb. We are accustomed to women in our society sharing in equal voting rights, equal civil rights, equal legal rights, equal labor rights...equality in every legal way.

This was not at all the case in the first century. Women had virtually none of these rights. In fact, a woman's testimony wasn't even allowed in court. Women were not just seen as second-class citizens, they were seen as second-rate humans.

It's absolutely remarkable that the writers of the gospel accounts include them in their story. If you were trying to make a fictional story sound real, if you were trying to sway your readers to believe in a story that you knew was false, if you were attempting to promote a resurrection/empty tomb story among skeptics, you most certainly *would not* build much of your story around the testimony of women. You might include the mayor, or powerful businessmen, or religious leaders, or just about anyone else. The only reason a writer would include women in such a story is if that story just happened to be *true.*

All four gospel writers give an account (though they vary slightly) of Mary, the mother of Jesus, and Mary Magdalene (whom Jesus had healed) as the first ones to discover the open tomb and the first ones to see the resurrected Jesus. Here is Matthew the tax collector's account:

> *"Early on Sunday morning, as the new day was dawning, Mary Magdalene and the other Mary went out to visit the tomb. Suddenly there was a great earthquake! For an angel of the Lord came down from heaven, rolled aside the stone, and sat on it. His face shone like lightning, and his clothing was as white as snow. The guards shook with fear when they saw him, and they fell into a dead faint. Then the angel spoke to the women. "Don't be afraid!" he said. "I know you are looking for Jesus, who was crucified. He isn't here! He is risen from the dead, just as he said would happen. Come, see where his body was lying. And now, go quickly and tell his disciples that he has risen from the dead, and he is going ahead of you to Galilee. You will see him there. Remember*

> *what I have told you." The women ran quickly from the tomb. They were very frightened but also filled with great joy, and they rushed to give the disciples the angel's message. And as they went, Jesus met them and greeted them. And they ran to him, grasped his feet, and worshiped him."*
> *Matthew 28:1-9*

If you were attempting to promote a resurrection/ empty tomb story among skeptics in the first century, you most certainly would not build much of your story around the testimony of women, unless that story was true.

The reality is that the gospel writers were not trying to strengthen a fictional story. They were simply writing a historical account of what actually happened.

The Romans

By their own admission, the tomb was empty.

The Roman and Jewish authorities knew they had killed a popular figure. They went to great lengths and took every precaution to make sure they squashed this carpenter's revolution and sent his band of followers back to the ordinary lives they came from. So after Jesus's death, they made sure none of his followers were able to continue his teachings.

> *The next day, on the Sabbath, the leading priests and Pharisees went to see Pilate. They told him, "Sir, we remember what that deceiver once said while he was still alive: 'After three days I will rise from the dead.' So we request that you seal the tomb until the third day. This*

> *will prevent his disciples from coming and stealing his body and then telling everyone he was raised from the dead! If that happens, we'll be worse off than we were at first." Pilate replied, "Take guards and secure it the best you can." So they sealed the tomb and posted guards to protect it. Matthew 27: 62-66*

These Roman guards were under threat of death to stand their post with vigilance. The Roman army was the most highly trained and disciplined military force of its day. They were the equivalent of our Army Rangers. If a Roman guard was found asleep or negligent in his duties, the punishment was death. That makes the next events quite noteworthy.

> *"As the women were on their way, some of the guards went into the city and told the leading priests what had happened. A meeting with the elders was called, and they decided to give the soldiers a large bribe. They told the soldiers, "You must say, 'Jesus' disciples came during the night while we were sleeping, and they stole his body.' If the governor hears about it, we'll stand up for you so you won't get in trouble." So the guards accepted the bribe and said what they were told to say. Their story spread widely among the Jews, and they still tell it today." Matthew 28:11-15*

This cover-up led to the "stolen body" theory, which we will discuss in a moment. While many lie for what they believe and even die for what they believe, what you don't see is people dying for what they know is false. As the saying goes, "Liars don't make martyrs."

The most reasonable story is that the Roman and Jewish government both concede that the tomb is empty and then they try to cover up how it became empty.

People don't die for what they know to be false. Liars don't make martyrs.

The Prophets

Long before the disciples, James, Paul, or the women came on the scene, there were men speaking of a coming Messiah. These prophecies add tremendous credibility to what the eye-witnesses describe about the life of Jesus.

In all of history, who fits the following criteria and what are the odds that *anyone* could fit the criteria by accident?

1. Seed of a Woman — Genesis 3:15
2. Seed of Abraham — Genesis 12: 3,7
3. Tribe of Judah — Genesis 49:10
4. Lineage of David — Jeremiah 23:5,6
5. Born in Bethlehem — Micah 5:2
6. God and Man — Isaiah 9:6
7. Visits the Temple — Malachi 3:1
8. Dies a sacrificial death — Isaiah 53: 1- 10
9. Rises from the dead — Isaiah 53:11

The odds of all these prophecies coming true arbitrarily by chance are equivalent to covering the state of Texas with silver dollars up to your knees, with a single coin painted red, and then walking across the state blindfolded, stopping anywhere you choose, digging through the coins, and finding the single red one among the pile.

Combining the uncannily accurate prophecies about Jesus with the eyewitness accounts of His life can really only lead to one reasonable conclusion: Jesus was far more than a man. He was exactly who He claimed to be, and His resurrection is the stamp of authority on all He taught and who He is.

The paper trail is very clear. The vast amount of documentation we have on the life of Jesus dwarfs every other work of antiquity. Its quantity, reliability, and authenticity gives us evidence beyond a reasonable doubt that Jesus was far more than just a man.

Before we move on, let's boil this down…

The Top Nine Reasons we know the NT writers tell the truth about Jesus:

9. They embarrass themselves.
8. They include embarrassing details about Jesus.
7. They include harsh and demanding sayings of Jesus.
6. More than thirty people whose historical existence is confirmed are mentioned in the writings.
5. Divergent details. These stories are not copy/paste versions. These differences add personal eyewitness authenticity.
4. They challenge readers to check out their facts.

3. Unembellished simple historical writing. The New Testament does not bear any similarities to mythical or legend writing. It is simple, historical documentation.
2. They include resurrection events they wouldn't have invented.
1. Immediately after Jesus' death, *none* of them believed he was the Messiah.

After the crucifixion, Jesus' followers were scared, dejected, and disappointed. They were hiding from authorities, knowing their hopes for a revolution were over. They were not confident, expectant, and hopeful, waiting at the tomb for Jesus' promise of a resurrection to come true. The fact is, they didn't believe it would come true. They didn't believe it until *after* they saw him.

> *For me personally, this is one of the most powerful truths that led me to accept the resurrection as historically accurate. None of the disciples believed Jesus was the Christ immediately after He was killed.*

All these facts confirm that Jesus really did rise from the dead and debunk the popular anti-resurrection conspiracies. There are still those who reject the abundant evidence and create wild theories to explain the resurrection. It's not hard to disprove those theories.

1. Stolen body theory

The logistics needed to pull this off are very difficult to believe. The grieving followers of Jesus, supposedly motivated by a desire to keep his revolution going, had to "fulfill" his resurrection prophecy. They overpowered the armed Roman guards and then unsealed the cemented stone. Then they rolled away a rock weighing several tons. Then they smuggled the corpse away and hid it and began proclaiming a message of resurrection they knew was a lie. For argument's sake, let's pretend they did accomplish this amazing feat, which is worthy of a "Mission Impossible" scene. The big question is still…why? Why would they feel the need to perpetuate a story they themselves knew wasn't true? To what end? For what gain? All they got out of it was more scrutiny, more pressure, more discomfort, and, for many, death. It doesn't make any sense. What's ironic here is that after they saw the empty tomb, even *they* thought someone took the body. It wasn't an empty tomb that sparked a revolution — it was a resurrected savior.

2. Romans hid the body

This conspiracy theory suggests that to prevent the disciples from stealing the body, the Roman authorities stored it away. Considering that the disciples began proclaiming the resurrection story soon after this, the hid-the-body theory doesn't make sense. If the Romans hid the corpse, they would have immediately produced it when the church gained influence. The church didn't start with the amazing story of a missing body. The early church was ignited with the story of a resurrected Savior. It's not that they *didn't see* a dead body, it's that they *did see* a live one.

3. Swoon theory

Jesus didn't really die, but simply passed out and then came to. This theory misses so much. The Romans were expert executioners and had crucified thousands of victims. They knew exactly what they were doing and had pronounced Jesus dead. This theory doesn't explain the historical accounts. How'd the stone get moved? There's no historical account of Jesus living after that. How do you explain Paul's testimony? There are too many holes for this theory to have any credibility.

4. Hallucination theory

There are no recorded accounts in all of history of "group hallucinations." One person, in great grief, may have such an experience, but hundreds of people at different times… no. This theory doesn't explain the empty tomb, nor does it explain the conversion of the skeptic, James, or of the enemy, Paul.

5. Wrong Tomb

Much like the "Romans-hid-the-body" theory, this one misses the point altogether. It's not that the disciples saw an empty tomb and reported Jesus was alive. They saw an empty tomb, then a *resurrected Jesus,* and *knew* He was alive. Conspiracy theorists miss the point when they try to explain away the empty tomb. An empty tomb is not the issue. It's the hundreds of eyewitnesses of a resurrected Jesus and the incredible transformation that subsequently took place that must be explained. As with many others, this doesn't explain why James, the skeptic, and then later, Paul, the enemy, both became followers.

6. Disciples' faith led to their resurrection belief

Again, this does *not* agree with the historical evidence we have. Jesus' followers testified to their fear and disbelief. This is one of the reasons we know their stories are authentic. They included so many embarrassing details about themselves. They weren't filled with faith, but fear, right after Jesus was killed. We don't see any evidence of faith until *after* they claim to have seen Jesus. Resurrection led to faith, not vice versa.

7. New Testament writers simply copied pagan resurrection myths

This is the new flavor-of-the-month argument for resurrection skeptics. All the others have fallen by the wayside under the weight of the evidence and common sense. It sounds so enlightened and educated. Unfortunately for skeptics, this theory, like the others, holds no credibility.

Grasping at straws, the promoters of this theory contend that Christianity and Jesus are mirror images of older, pagan religions that include in their mythology blood sacrifice, resurrection, divine offspring being killed, and so on. Mythical stories involving Marduk, Osiris, and Adonis are often cited. While there may be some very general similarities, that's all there are. Today's scholars would not regard these stories as substantive or parallel and the earliest possible parallel is more than 100 years after Jesus.

The Jesus story reads as authentic historical accounts by eyewitnesses, while the pagan myths read just as that — myths. These myths are most often tied to annual cycles of planting and harvesting of crops. This life and death cycle is portrayed in the mythology for the worshipper to seek the god's blessing on their crops. While it does include the theme of life coming from death, the Jesus story has at its core an altogether different and deeper meaning. These opposing theories can't explain the evidence for Jesus' resurrection.

When we examine all of the historical and manuscript evidence, then weigh in the type of writing and the people making the eyewitness claims, there is really only one scenario that fits the evidence.

Jesus, who was born in Bethlehem to descendants of David and grew up in Nazareth, had a huge following and was killed for his teachings. His body was placed in a tomb owned by one of the known religious leaders. The stone was cemented in place and Roman guards were set at watch under threat of death if they failed in their duty. Three days later, the tomb was empty, the enormous stone was dislodged, and angelic sightings were reported. While the timid, faithless disciples huddled in fear, Jesus sightings began to occur. Jesus bodily appeared in several different locations to hundreds of his followers, including his brother, a lifelong skeptic. Most of these people were still alive when documented teachings of His resurrection began to circulate. Later, the risen Jesus appeared to Paul, the enemy of the church. All of these witnesses had dramatic, life altering transformations that impacted their behavior for the rest of their lives. Many of them died for what they reported they saw.

The only reasonable scenario that fits all those facts is that Jesus was more than a teacher. He was exactly who He claimed to be. He *is* the prophesied Messiah, He *did* rise from the dead, and He *is* the God revealed in the Bible.

Unlike other prophets, Jesus doesn't give us the "good guy, moral teacher" option to explain his identity. His words are too outlandish. "Before Abraham was I am." "I am the way, the truth, and the life." "If you have seen the Father, you have seen me." "I and the father are one." "Your sins are forgiven." You either have to take him at his words or reject him as a crazy person. C.S.

Lewis in his classic, Mere Christianity, states it far better than I ever could.

> *"I am trying to prevent anyone saying the really foolish things that people often say about Him. "I'm ready to accept Jesus as a great moral teacher, but I don't accept His claim to be God. That is the one thing we must not say. A man who was merely a man and said the sort of things Jesus said would not be a great moral teacher. He would rather be a lunatic — on a level with the man who says he is a poached egg —or else the devil of hell. You must make your choice. Either this man was, and is, the Son of God: or else a madman or something worse. You can shut him up for a fool, you can spit at Him and kill Him as a demon, or you can fall at His feet and call Him Lord and God. But let us not come with any patronizing nonsense about His being a great human teacher. He has not left that open to us. He did not intend to." — C.S. Lewis* [8]

The evidence is pretty clear. Though each singular piece might be explained away, as a whole it paints a very compelling picture. Jesus' life was foretold by the prophets, born of a virgin, taught his followers that he was God, died a sacrificial death, and then rose again to cover our sins, all just as he said. When we take into consideration the amount of power needed to create the entire universe and bring life out of nothing, it's not a leap of faith at all to believe that he could also rise from the dead.

Now pull back a bit and take a big view of His impact.

"He was born in an obscure village the child of a peasant. He grew up in another village, where he worked in a carpenter shop until he was thirty. Then, for three years, he was an itinerant preacher.

He never wrote a book. He never held an office. He never had a family or owned a home. He didn't go to college. He never lived in a big city. He never traveled 200 miles from the place where he was born. He did none of the things that usually accompany greatness. He had no credential but himself.

He was only thirty-three when the tide of public opinion turned against him. His friends ran away. One of them denied him. He was turned over to his enemies and went through a mockery of a trial. He was nailed to a cross between two thieves. While he was dying, his executioners gambled for his garment, the only property he had on Earth. When he was dead, he was laid in a borrowed grave, through the pity of a friend.

Twenty centuries have come and gone, and today he is the central figure of the human race. I am well within the mark when I say that all the armies that ever marched, all the navies that ever sailed, all the parliaments that ever sat, all the kings that ever reigned — put together — have not affected the life of man on this Earth as much as that one, solitary life."

— One Solitary Life

The overwhelming evidence from the eyewitnesses to Jesus' life and ministry show beyond reasonable doubt that Jesus was no ordinary man and his life was no ordinary life. God came in human form, just as the prophets said, taught us how to treat each other, and died a sacrificial death to pay for our sins. His resurrection proves that he is exactly who he said he was.

Conclusion

We have explored an enormous amount of material in the last few pages. Let's wrap it up with a review.

The size, scope and origin of the universe reveals that God exists as an *immaterial, uncaused, timeless, powerful, Creator.*

The well-ordered make-up and fine-tuning of the universe points to a creator that is a *volitional thinker* and an *intelligent designer.*

The complexity of life and the biological information carrier, DNA, shows that God, not natural random processes, is a *life-giver.*

The ethical codes demonstrated by people everywhere reveal that God is a *moral, rational being.*

The above evidence, combined with *Occham's Razor,* rules out all religions, except monotheistic ones, as the religions that could reveal a more detailed description of the Creator.

The *timing, nature,* and *volume* of manuscripts of the New Testament demonstrate that it is supremely reliable to accurately tell of the events it contains.

The *reliability* of the New Testament, and the *eye witness accounts* of the life, death, and resurrection of Jesus (along with the OT prophecies that his life fulfills) proves beyond reasonable doubt that Jesus was far more than just a historical figure, but actually *God in the flesh.*

SUMMARY

The God that creation reveals is described accurately in the Christian Bible. While creation reveals some of His characteristics, the story He left us reveals far more of His character. The theme of that story is the scarlet thread of redemption and love, culminating in the personal sacrifice for our sins. The timeless, powerful, uncaused, intelligent, life-giver sacrificed Himself on the cross, then rose from the dead so that we could have an eternal relationship with Him. In doing so, He completed His entire purpose in creation — to be with us.

Please allow that to sink in. The God of the universe created everything to be with you. Then fully embrace the human experience so that He could enjoy your company — forever. This was always His goal — the main point. *You* are the main point.

Creation and the resurrection both have the same goal in mind — to bring humanity into a relationship with the Creator. Through creation, God brings us to life physically and through the resurrection, God brings us to life spiritually.

You are the main point of creation and the main point of salvation. God created the universe, and you, so He could love you, and Jesus died and rose again to save you. You are His greatest masterpiece.

The resurrection is the apex moment in all of history. Everything before that weekend looks toward it and everything since looks back on it. The God of the universe came down in human form to show us a way to Him. He then died to cover the chasm between us so we could have the relationship He has designed us for.

It's an amazing, profound love story. This is no fairy tale, however. This love story is deeply rooted in history and can be embraced with great certainty.

Final Thoughts

I hope this has been a worthwhile journey for you. Thank you for taking the time to join me in your own process of discovery. Even if you don't agree with my conclusions, thank you for your open mindedness and willingness to consider the evidence. Each time I read through the growing mountain of evidence, I'm more persuaded away from my previous agnostic world-view and more drawn to the reality of God's existence. I'm continually in awe that God not only exists —that's pretty clear — but that He loves us so much. He wants to be known. We were not created simply to exist, but to experience Him. I can only hope that the previous pages will do more than just unlock in you an intellectual agreement that there is a Creator, but deeper than that, I hope it sparks a personal, intimate, growing relationship with Him. I hope your journey does not stop with the closing of these pages, but continues on as you get to know Him more fully. In doing so, you will also uncover the best version of who you were created to be.

Keep asking questions. He is waiting to be discovered.

—HR

Chapter Footnotes

Chapter 2

1. Hick, John. "Debate on the Existence of God." *The Existence of God*. New York: Macmillan, 1964. 175. Print.
2. Hereen, Fred. *Show Me God.* Wheeling: Daystar, 2000. 157. Print.
3. Albert Einstein in an oral response to a question about his theory of General Relativity.
4. Ross, Hugh. *The Creator and the Cosmos.* Colorado Springs: NavPress, 1995. 19. Print.
5. Hereen, Fred. *Show Me God.* Wheeling: Daystar, 2000. 168. Print.
6. Barrow, John and Frank Tipler. *The Anthropic Cosmological Principle.* Oxford: University Press, 1986. 442. Print
7. Davies Paul. *The Cosmic Blueprint.* New York: Simon & Shuster, 1988. 20. Print.
8. Bazarov, *Thermodynamics.* Pergamon. 1964. Print.
9. Jastrow, Robert. *God and the Astronomers.* Readers Library, 2000. 16. Print.
10. Jastrow, Robert. *God and the Astronomers.* Readers Library, 2000. 14. Print.
11. Jastrow, Robert. "A Scientist Caught Between Two Faiths: Interview with Robert Jastrow." *Christianity Today* 6 Aug. 1982. Print.

Chapter 3

1. Craig, William Lane and Quentin Smith. *Theism, Atheism and Big Bang Cosmology.* Oxford: Oxford University Press, 1995. 135. Print.
2. *Oxford Dictionary.* Oxford: Oxford University Press, 2014. Print.
3. Bacon, Francis. *Novum Organum,* 1620.
4. Personal letter to John Stewart, 1754.

Chapter 4

1. Hereen, Fred. *Show Me God.* Wheeling: Daystar, 2000. 135. Print.
2. Newton, Issac. General Scholium. Translated by Motte, A. 1825. *Newton's Principia: The Mathematical Principles of Natural Philosophy.* New York: Daniel Adee. 501. Print.
3. Hoyle, Fred and Nalin Chandra Wickramasinghe. *Evolution from Space.* Touchstone. 1981. 148, 150. Print.
4. Jastrow, Robert. *God and the Astronomers.* Readers Library, 2000. 116. Print.

Chapter 5

1. Strobel, Lee. *The Case for a Creator: A Journalist Investigates Scientific Evidence That Points Toward God.* Grand Rapids: Zondervan, 2004. Print.
2. Weinberg, Steven. *A Designer Universe? New York Review of Books.* 21 Oct, 1999. Print.

3. Weinberg, Steven. *A Designer Universe? New York Review of Books.* 21 Oct, 1999. Print.
4. Strobel, Lee. *The Case for a Creator: A Journalist Investigates Scientific Evidence That Points Toward God.* Grand Rapids: Zondervan, 2004. 178. Print.
5. Sagan, Carl. *Pale Blue Dot.* New York: Ballantine, 1994. 7. Print.
6. Davis, and Harry L. Poe. *Designer Universe.* Nashville: Broadman & Holman, 2002. 107. Print.
7. Davis, Jimmy H. and Harry L. Poe. *Designer Universe.* Nashville: Broadman & Holman, 2002. 107. Print.
8. Jastrow, Robert. *God and the Astronomers.* Readers Library, 2000. 118. Print.
9. Ross, Hugh. *The Creator and the Cosmos, 3rd ed.* Colorado Springs: NavPress, 2001. 224. Print.
10. Davies, Paul. *Superforce: The Search for a Grand Unified Theory of Nature.* New York: Simon and Schuster, 1984. 235-236. Print.
11. Glynn, Patrick. *God: The Evidence: The Reconciliation of Faith and Reason in a Postsecular World.* New York: Crown, 1999. 55. Print.

Chapter 6

1. Leslie, John. *Universes.* Abingdon: Routledge, 1989. 304. Print.
2. Davies, Paul. *The Mind of God.* New York: Touchstone, 1992. 16, 232. Print.
3. Hereen, Fred. *Show Me God,* vol. 1. Wheeling: Daystar, 2000. 239. Print.

4. Easterbrook, Gregg. "The New Convergence." *Wired.* Dec 2002. Print.
5. Strobel, Lee. *The Case for Faith.* Grand Rapids: Zondervan, 2000. 78, 79. Print.
6. Strobel, Lee. *The Case for a Creator: A Journalist Investigates Scientific Evidence That Points Toward God.* Grand Rapids: Zondervan, 2004. 145, 146. Print.
7. Dembski, William A. and James M. Kushiner. *Signs of Intelligence.* 170. Print.
8. Smith, *Atheism.* Amherst: Prometheus, 1989. 239. Print.
9. Leslie, John. *Universes.* Abingdon: Routledge, 1989. 198. Print.
10. Augros, and George N. Stanciu. *The New Story of Science.* New York: Bantam, 1986. 70. Print.

Chapter 8

1. Mc Kean, Kevin. *Discover,* no. 189. 7. Print.
2. Chen, J. P. and C. T. "Photochemistry of Methane, Nitrogen, and Water Mixture As a Model for the Atmosphere of the Primitive Earth." *Journal of American Chemical Society,* vol. 97:11. 1975. 2964. Print.
3. Bliss, Richard B., Gary E. Parker, Duane T. Gish. *Origin of Life,* 3rd ed. California: C.L.P. Publications, 1990. 14-15. Print.
4. "Life's Crucible." *Earth* Feb. 1998: 34. Print.
5. Bird, *The Origin of Species Revisited.* Nashville: Thomas Nelson Co., 1991. 325. Print. Emphasis mine.
6. Darwin, Charles. *On the Origin of Species.* 1839. 490. Print.
7. Darwin, Charles. *On the Origin of Species.* 1839. 5. Print.
8. Darwin, Charles. *The Origin of Species: A Facsimile of the First Edition.* Boston: Harvard University Press, 1964. 179. Print.

9. Darwin, Charles. *The Origin of Species by Means of Natural Selection.* New York: Random House. 124-125. Print.
10. George, T. Neville. "Fossils in Evolutionary Perspective." *Science Progress,* vol. 48. Jan. 1960. 1, 3. Print.
11. Eldredge, N. and I. Tattersall. *The Myths of Human Evolution.* New York: Columbia University Press, 1982. 59. Print.
12. Jay Gould, Stephen. "An Asteroid to Die For." *Discover.* Oct. 1989. 65. Print.
13. Dawkins, Richard. *The Blind Watchmaker.* London: W.W. Norton & Company, 1987. 229. Print.
14. Muggeridge, Malcolm. *The End of Christendom.* Grand Rapids: Eerdmans, 1980. 59. Print.
15. Jay Gould, Stephen. "Smith Woodward's Folly." *New Scientist.* 5 Apr, 1979. 43. Print.
16. Gregory, William K. "Hesperopithecus Apparently Not An Ape Nor A Man." *Science,* vol. 66, issue 1720. 16 Dec, 1927. 579. Print.
17. Jay Gould, Stephen. "Abscheulich! Atrocious!" *Natural History.* Mar. 2002. Print.

Chapter 9

1. Johnson, George Sim. "Did Darwin Get It Right?" *The Wall Street Journal.* 15 Oct, 1999. Print.
2. Denton, Michael. *Evolution: A Theory in Crisis.* London: Burnett Books, 1985. 334. Print.
3. Horgan, John. "In the Beginning." *Scientific American,* vol. 264. Feb. 1991. 119. Print.
4. E. Orgel, Leslie. "The Origin of Life on Earth." *Scientific American,* vol. 271. Oct. 1994. 78. Print.

5. Crick, Francis. *Life Itself: It's Origin and Nature.* New York: Simon & Schuster, 1981. 88. Print.
6. Denton, Michael. *Evolution: A Theory in Crisis.* London: Burnett Books, 1985. 351. Print.
7. Alberts, Bruce. "The Cell as a Collection of Protein Machines: Preparing the Next Generation of Molecular Biologists." *Cell,* 92. 8 Feb, 1998. 291. Print.
8. Salisbury, Frank. "Doubts About the Modern Synthetic Theory of Evolution." *American Biology Teacher.* Sep. 1971. 338. Print.
9. Wells, Jonathan. *Icons of Evolution: Science or Myth? Why Much of What We Teach About Evolution is Wrong.* Washington, D.C.: Regnery, 2000. 221. Print.
10. Strobel, Lee. *The Case for Faith.* Grand Rapids: Zondervan, 2000. 108. Print.

Chapter 10

1. Neal, Meghan. *Motherboard.* 7 Aug. 2013. Web.
2. Penfield, Wilder. *The Mystery of the Mind.* Princeton: Princeton University Press, 1975. xiii. Print.
3. Penfield, Wilder. *The Mystery of the Mind.* Princeton: Princeton University Press, 1975. 77-78. Print.
4. Ropeik, David. *How Risky Is It, Really?* Psychology Today. 27 Dec, 2011.
5. Witham, Larry. *By Design.* 211 Print.
6. Hackett, *The Reconstruction of the Christian Revelation Claim.* Grand Rapids: Baker, 1984. 111. Print.

CHAPTER 11

1. Lewis, C.S. *Mere Christianity.* New York: Macmillan, 1952. 19. Print.
2. Geisler, Norman L. and Frank Turek. *I Don't Have Enough Faith to be an Atheist.* Wheaton: Crossway Books, 2004. Print.
3. Wilson, and Michael Ruse. *The Evolution of Ethics.* 1991. Print.
4. Hitler, Adolf. *Mein Kampf,* vol. 1, chapter XI. Print.
5. Darwin, Charles. *The Descent of Man,* 1871. Print.
6. Keith, Arthur. *Evolution and Ethics.* Putnam, 1947. 230. Print.

CHAPTER 12

1. Young, William Paul. *Crossroads.* New York: FaithWords, 2012. 153-154. Print.

CHAPTER 14

1. Josephus. *Antiquities.* 18:3:3. Print.
2. Josephus. *Antiquities.* 20:9:1. Print.
3. Geisler, Norman L. *Baker Encyclopedia of Christian Apologetics.* Grand Rapids: Baker, 1999. 381-385. Print.
4. Habermas, and Michael R. Licona. *The Case for the Resurrection of Jesus.* Grand Rapids: Kregel, 2004. 23. Print.
5. Habermas, Gary R. and Michael R. Licona. *The Case for the Resurrection of Jesus.* Grand Rapids: Kregel, 2004. Print.
6. Geisler, Norman and Frank Turek. *I Don't Have Enough Faith to be an Atheist.* Wheaton: Crossway Books, 2004. 223. Print.

7. McDowell, Josh. *A Ready Defense.* Nashville: Thomas Nelson, 1993. 45. Print.
8. Lewis, C.S. *Mere Christianity.* London: Collins, 1952. 54 – 56. Print.

Appendix

Detailed Outline of the Questions

III. Question 2 — Why is There Something Rather Than Nothing?

Chapter 2 **page 19**

A. Explanation 1 - The Universe is Eternal

1. The B.E.G.I.N. scientific facts that prove this false.
    a. Background Radiation proves the reality of the "Big Bang" explosion.
    b. Einstein's theory of general relativity shows the mathematical model that time and space had a singular point of beginning.
    c. Galaxy seeds reveal the early formation of the galaxies and the "fingerprint of the maker."
    d. The inflating universe and the Doppler shift of light proved Einstein's mathematical predictions to be correct. Everything in the universe is moving away from everything else.
    e. eNergy depletion and the second law of thermodynamics proves the universe couldn't be infinitely old or it would have run out of energy an infinite time ago.

Chapter 3 **page 41**

B. Explanation 2 - The Universe is Self-Existent

The Kalam Cosmological argument uses logic and experience to prove this explanation false.

1. Everything that has a beginning must have a cause outside of itself.
2. The universe had a beginning.

3. Therefore, the universe must have a cause outside of itself.

Chapter 4 **page 51**

C. Explanation 3 - The Universe is Created
If the universe is not eternal and couldn't create itself, it only stands to reason it must have a cause outside of itself — namely a creator.

IV. Question 3 — Why is There Order and Not Chaos?

Chapter 5 - Evidences of Design **page 59**

A. An illustration from a pioneer rock home shows the improbability of order emerging from randomness.
B. The incredibly precise nature of gravity is just one of the finely tuned mechanisms that allows for life on Earth. If moved in either direction life would be impossible.
C. The cosmological constant, the energy density of empty space, is incredibly well adjusted and "inconceivably precise."
D. Carbon production in the stars is a very well ordered and consistent process. Carbon is the basis of all of life, and this production makes all life possible.
E. While once thought to be nothing more than an ordinary star, our sun is now seen to be quite extraordinary in many ways. Its highly unusual properties make our sun very rare.
F. Earth is much more than just a speck of dust in the universe. In fact, it is extremely well designed. The

odds are that the earth is so rare that it is most likely the only one of its kind in the entire universe.

Chapter 6 - Explanations of Design **page 81**

A. The "Just-the-way-it-is" theory or "brute facts" argument states that life stems from just those conditions and that's why life happens to be on this planet. We shouldn't try to find an explanation, it's "just the way it is." We would never accept this argument in any other realm of life when enormously high odds are consistently beaten.
B. The Multiverse verse hypothesis recognizes the enormity of the odds that have to be beaten for there to be life on Earth, so the proponents of this theory simply propose that there are an almost infinite number of universes and we just happen to be in the one where all the right conditions came together. There is one major flaw with this theory — there is absolutely no evidence for it.

V. Question 4 — Why is There Life?

Chapter 8 - Natural Explanations **page 99**

A. For life to evolve, it had to begin. The now discredited Miller experiments prove that producing life from non-living chemicals is monumentally difficult. Atheists believe that what intelligent beings can't do in a safe laboratory happened by accident on a hostile Earth.

B. Macro-evolution, or the transmutation of species, is the typical natural explanation for the variety of life on Earth. This process is based on two functions.
   1. Mutation
      Offspring is slightly genetically different from the parent.
   2. Natural Selection
      Survival of the fittest decides which of these mutations will be passed on to the next generation.

C. Though we can easily see evolution within a species the fossil record simply doesn't show the evidence for long chain of countless mutations leading from one species to another. If this was the actual reason for life on Earth the fossil record would look very different.

D. Hoaxes: The "Piltdown man," "Nebraska man," and Haeckel's embryos were great hoaxes played on the public to try to get us to believe what the real evidence fails to show. This is further proof that scientists often substitute their worldview for real science.

Chapter 9 – Evidences of Supernatural Creation page 121

A. The DNA molecule is a powerful piece of evidence for divine design. Information comes from intelligence. This is true of Shakespeare's Hamlet, a computer binary code, or a biological code that instructs the body to manufacture proteins.

B. The human body is a finely-tuned, well-ordered manufacturing plant. The biological machinery inside the human cell is incredibly well made. If we saw this level of production efficiency anywhere else we would immediately assume an intelligent source.

C. Common descent or common design? Many look to the commonalities across species as proof for common descent. But we can look at many designed things, airplanes for example, and show that intelligent design will also lead to a common look.

VI. Question 5 — How Am I Aware?

Chapter 10 **page 141**

A. One part or two? Are we purely a physical body and nothing more, or is there evidence that, in addition to our brain, we also have a mind?
   1. The Montreal Procedure, and many other experiments, show conclusively that our mind is certainly connected to our brain, but they are not one and the same. We have mental functions that are outside of our brain.
   2. Dreams are another example of the mind working independently of the brain. Dreamers are the only one that can describe a dream.

B. The mind and God. If we are an immaterial being housed in a physical body that is yet another piece of evidence for an immaterial creator that created all things physical.

VII. Question 6 — Why Do I Care?

Chapter 11 **page 159**

A. Moral law is irrefutable. Morality and a sense of right and wrong are seen in every culture in every age in history. Even the relativist, who claims there really is no such thing as absolute morality, will act very differently when his person or property is violated. What he claims in theory he rejects in reality.

B. Some would like to credit social evolution with our sense of morality, justice and compassion. While treating those who can do us great good may fit this theory, the fact that we show such characteristics to strangers and the weak proves that survival of the fittest can't explain compassion.

C. Adolf Hitler and Mother Theresa are good examples of the tension for the belief of morality. Hitler is a perfect example of how one should act if evolution was true, and yet he is universally reviled. The saint from Calcutta should be seen as a fool by those who reject God, and yet even those who deny theism praise her works.

D. Shaeffer's two story house is a wonderful word picture of how the atheist rejects the source of the theist's world of beauty, compassion, kindness and justice but yet refuses to live in any other world.

VIII. Question 7 — Why is There So Much Pain?

Chapter 12 **page 183**

A. Many may argue that pain and suffering are all the proof they need that a good God doesn't exist. The truth is that most of our pain in life comes from the incredible power of poor choices. We are given the gift of choice because the creator wants us to love freely. Love and pain are the two sides of the same coin of choice.

B. The bigger picture reveals that while great pain comes from choice, great beauty, incredible sacrifice, and inspiring stories also stem from that same gift of choice. Pain can produce unbelievable beauty, like a bulb that leads to a beautiful flower.

IX. Question 8 — Do All Religions Lead to God?

Chapter 13 **page 201**

A. The four blind monk analogy fails to show that different religions all lead to the same God. It is a self-defeating argument because the teller of the analogy assumes an all-seeing vantage point and has a gross misunderstanding of the nature of religions.

B. While we live in a pluralistic society and enjoy the freedom of valuing every person, this does not mean every belief system has equal merit. Just believing something passionately does not make it true, and two mutually exclusive truths can't both be right.

C. Atheism is ruled out by the vast amount of evidence that makes a belief in God very reasonable.

D. All pantheistic religions don't fit the evidence because the creator can't be part of the created universe. The evidence shows that the creator must be separate and apart from the creation.

E. Karma doesn't fit the evidence either. The universe is clearly well thought out and designed. An impersonal force doesn't explain the complexity of information codes, biological machines, and a well-ordered universe.

F. Occam's Razor is used to by detectives everywhere to shave away unnecessary explanations for a set of evidences. This same logical principle can be used to eliminate all polytheistic religions, such as Hinduism. There is no need to believe in multiple eternal, self-existent, powerful, timeless, immaterial beings when one will fit the evidence perfectly.

G. All this evidence leads us to the three major monotheistic religions: Islam, Judaism, and Christianity. It all really boils down to whether Jesus is God or not.

X. Question 9 — Is Jesus Really God?

Chapter 14 **page 221**

A. There are several historical references outside of the Bible that prove that Jesus really lived. If those are rejected, then the existence of Tiberius Caesar needs to be rejected as well.

B. The New Testament is the most supported document in all of history.

1. The quantity of documentation dwarfs all other well received ancient documents. If the New Testament is rejected as authentic then all the works of Aristotle, Socrates, Plato and even Homer should be rejected as well.
2. The dating of the New Testament documentation is also far superior to all the works of antiquity mentioned above.

C. The New Testament is not just trustworthy based on the quantity and dating of the documents, but the content of what is recorded is trustworthy as well because of who documented the events and why.

1. The disciples wrote down what they witnessed and experienced. They had nothing to gain and everything to lose by fabricating a myth. The evidence shows that they did not believe Jesus was God until after they saw Him risen.
2. Jesus' skeptical brother James did not believe Jesus was the Messiah. Only the resurrection is a good explanation for his changed belief and behavior.
3. Paul was a staunch enemy of the early church but radically changed his message after a personal experience with the risen Jesus. Only such an experience can explain his transformation.
4. The Gospel writers all documented that women were the first on the scene at the empty tomb. Given the legal standing of women in the culture at that time, no writer would include such details unless they were historically accurate.

5. The many prophesies from the Old Testament add another layer of credibility to the resurrection story. It's mathematically impossible for all these facts to come to pass on accident.
6. None of the handful of alternate theories for the resurrection stand up to the evidence.
    a. The stolen body theory doesn't account for the actual sightings by a large number of people.
    b. The theory that the Romans hid the body also doesn't account for the sightings by the disciples, James or Paul. Nor does it explain why the Romans didn't produce the body when the resurrection story became popular.
    c. The swoon theory doesn't account for the reliability of the death certification nor the rolled away stone.
    d. The hallucination theory is farfetched at best. There are no mass hallucinations in history. It still doesn't account for the conversion of James, the skeptic or Paul, the enemy.
    e. The wrong tomb theory, much like the stolen body theory, misses the point that it wasn't an empty tomb that launched Christianity, it was a risen Jesus.
    f. The disciples' faith did not lead them to write of a mythical resurrection. In fact, they had no faith that Jesus would rise from the dead. They were afraid and hidden away. They only became emboldened world changers after they witnessed a resurrected Jesus.

g. The gospel writers did not copy from pagan mythology for their resurrection story. Those pagan myths bear little or no resemblance to the historical writing of the New Testament authors. The closest parallel doesn't come until 100 years after Jesus' resurrection.
h. The only story line that fits all the evidence is that Jesus is the prophesied Messiah from the Old Testament. He is God in the flesh, just as He proclaimed. The many eyewitnesses to His resurrection give the stamp of authenticity that He is exactly who He claimed to be. Jesus is more than a carpenter, teacher, or prophet. The most reasonable conclusion, given the evidence, is that the God of creation overcame death so that we could experience His grace, love and forgiveness. Jesus bodily rose from the dead to give us new life and promise His followers eternal life with Him.